P R

SAGE SAPIEN

Why live a one-note life through our mental faculties when we are so much more? Reading *Sage Sapien* by Johnson Chong, I rested in the peaceful shadow of a young dragon who presented a body of yogic wisdom through a modern lens. I trusted Johnson to delve deep into the river of my own consciousness and ride the current of his story to discover more about my own story, my own dharma. The articulate yet emotional explanations of Johnson's life experiences allowed me to understand my own life experiences at a deeper level. In an age of intellectual, emotional and spiritual confusion, Johnson provides a spiritual lens in the form of this book, for you to either make sense of that confusion or to make peace with it by accepting what is.

He highlights that "we are already enlightened, and we only forgot." *Sage Sapien* allows us to remember that which we have forgotten: that we are more than what our minds tell us we are. There are many more pieces of ourselves that have more power. I invite you to read this book, this map to a river of consciousness, that will allow you to seek, find and awaken those pieces.

—Dion Jensen, Author of *The Good News About PTSD*

This is a wonderfully honest coming out story, but it is also a spiritual autobiography of an actor and accomplished international yogi, meditation teacher, and retreat facilitator. The book captures both of these seemingly disparate sides, showing how they naturally fit together. Johnson Chong tells of his education as an actor, emphasizing the consciousness-expanding and psychotherapeutic effects of acting training. Deeper than his interest in acting and show business was his quest to discover the meaning of life. Raised in a Chinese-American family, he was early exposed to martial arts and qi-gong with their mystical overlay of energy dynamics in the mind and body. He grew up rebelling against religion, yet ironically it led him to delve into the spiritual practices that can be associated with religion (like yoga, meditation, bodywork, Reiki and shamanic-inspired practices). *Sage Sapien* recounts episodes during his training in these mind-body practices woven into a sort of travelogue; Chong has traveled and lived in India and Singapore and has collected universal truths from very wise teachers. In spite of the ethereal focuses in his life, his story sounds very down-to-earth and real.

I particularly appreciated the revelation of the spiritual side of his life. Scattered through the story are discussions of Jungian theory and archetypal patterns, astrology, karma, reincarnation, lessons on how to overcome suffering and how to find meaning in life. These are questions that all people—and I think, in a special way, gay people—ask, but that are usually left out of autobiographies because they're too personal. Chong is an earnest young gay man seeking to serve humanity, telling the truth about his experience, and pursuing whatever enlightenment has become in our modern era. I think spiritually-interested gay men (partly because we naturally see through traditional religions) are part of a vanguard in the evolution of consciousness to discover what "enlightenment" can mean today.

I found the book fast and easy reading. It left me hungry to know more about the author and how his life developed even further beyond the coming out to his parents that closes the story told in this volume. He does not say much about his current work and projects. His accomplishments, like the travel retreats he leads, are revealed mostly in the author bio. I also would have liked to learn more of his spiritual "discoveries," what all his training has taught him about truth. There's another book still to come out of this story, I suspect. As an author of a "spiritual autobiography", at age 35, I've had to revise and update several times over the seventy-plus years I've lived so I appreciate how such autobiographies demand sequels.

—Toby Johnson, Author of *Gay Spirituality: Gay Identity and the Transformation of Human Consciousness* and *Finding Your Own True Myth: What I Learned from Joseph Campbell* and other books and novels.

This incredibly inspiring autobiography from Johnson Chong takes us on a journey of how he transformed himself. From the rigidity and pain of growing up in the bounds of conservative Asian family doctrines, he has evolved into a modern day sage of strength, courage and authenticity.

Through the openness to explore the depths of his "Self" and push through the bounds of both societal beliefs and self-limiting beliefs, Johnson cleverly highlights how his resistances and struggles have become some of his biggest blessings. His upbringing and non-linear journey from his young adult to adult years led to a constant questioning and re-defining of his identity and role in the world. Through all the good and all the bad, he embraces each experience as having played a critical role in who he has become and is becoming.

Anyone who has struggled with their identity (sexual, cultural or otherwise), or stepping into their authentic power, will really connect with this book through real life stories and challenges. This is truly a heart-felt story that is filled with humor, joy, sadness, and ultimately transformation through the active choice of expanding one's own consciousness.

Many people will resonate with and through Johnson's experiences, as he weaves all the threads of the spiritual world from astrology, the ancient Vedas, yoga, shamanism and more.

I could not put this brilliantly scripted book down even for a minute. I simply loved reading it. It takes real guts to expose your story to the world in order to help those who feel lost in life's challenges. This masterpiece will undoubtedly inspire modern day seekers to continue seeking and embodying each of their unique truths.

—Geeta Vara, Author of *Ayurveda: Ancient Wisdom for Modern Wellbeing*

Sage Sapien: From Karma to Dharma tells an incredible true story of heartbreak and love, fear and adventure, rebelliousness and freedom, failure and success. Anyone embarking on their spiritual path would greatly benefit from this book. Johnson Chong's true life experience is the perfect example of a person taking their given circumstances and using it to propel them forward into a life of wellness and self-awareness. His book demonstrates the importance of putting the spiritual puzzle pieces together to create a life filled with real connection, then using those connections to change the world for the better.

While most memoirs are recounted from childhood to present day, Johnson tells his story from darkness to light, from suffering to freedom. This story is told in terms of lessons learned and moments of clarity, and it's fascinating to see a person's life through that lens. He lays out the thoughts, fears and complexities of life that go through our minds daily, and allows us to organize them and apply them to our own everyday lives. This unique storytelling is something to be admired, and I will certainly keep his lessons close to me as I continue on my own journey towards spiritual wellness.

—Ally Johnson, Radio Host of *Channel Q*, Creator of *Butch Pal for the Straight Gal*

In *Sage Sapien: From Kharma to Dharma*, Johnson Chong courageously shares his story in a captivating, generous and compassionate way. We follow a young boy, marginalised by society and lost in the world, to then connect with a young man who ventures out to discover himself and find his path. Chong shares his journey with all its ups and downs, and his experiences resonate deeply because they are very human. His journey to becoming a conscious, active and creative architect of his own healing and personal growth gives us hope and guidance.

Chong invites the reader to reflect on their own life through his life experiences. He uses his insights to help us grow in our own lives, to find our true paths and to hopefully lose some of the baggage that no longer serves us. I highly recommend this book for anyone who wants to discover their own truth, especially for those who have ever felt they don't belong.

—Amanda Thorpe, New Zealand

In this age of speed and impatience, reading Sage Sapien was a much needed slowing down, like savoring a cup of tea. It is calming, comforting and a huge sigh of relief. Johnson Chong's self-discovery process echoes my own personal ups and downs. I resonated very deeply with Johnson's childhood and upbringing, and reading his story allowed me to understand myself on a deeper level.

I particularly loved his message of encouraging us that "the sooner we realize that the purpose of life is to help each other untangle from the proverbial emotional luggage we came in with, the happier we will be." After finishing the book, it felt like I had time travelled into the past and retrieved a hidden part of myself that I had forgotten, but was always there. Essentially, I was inspired to fully be me, freely. This book is for people who are on a path of finding out who they truly are. So if you're ready to reconnect to the deepest parts of your soul, dust off your mind, and get yourself ready to meet yourself.

—Katie Chong, Hong Kong

Sage Sapien: From Karma to Dharma by Johnson Chong is written with true authenticity. Johnson bares his whole life experience to illustrate the conflicts of self-awareness, self-expression, self-acceptance, cultural and sexual identity and spiritual beliefs. Being raised in a traditional Chinese family in NYC, and then discovering his own sexuality, Johnson struggled tremendously. Along the way, he met people who showed him new perspectives in living his life that brought greater wisdom. Taking great courage to get uncomfortable, Johnson was able to become more self-aware and rediscover his true identity.

Embarking on a journey of yoga, meditation and alternative healing, Johnson was not only able to heal himself but also helped many others who faced similar struggles in life. The stories shared were so interesting that I could read them continuously for hours. I was so drawn into his imagery that I could feel myself being in the same space, traveling from America to India to Singapore and to China.

Every step of the way is an experience that is teaching us something we could benefit from, if we remember that everything in life happens for a reason. This is a good read for those who have always felt left of center, unique and often excluded from the majority. I highly recommend this book for anyone who is questioning their identity and seeking their truth, and also for those who desire to achieve inner peace in this messy, noisy world.

—Lowell Wang, Singapore

The journey of mind/emotional, physical and spiritual healing comes in many forms, and each person has his/her own unique path to finding wholeness. Author Johnson Chong shares his healing story in his memoir *Sage Sapien: From Karma to Dharma*. Chong has detailed his amazing journey in an authentic voice, including many moments of anger and rejection and then finding his way to self-acceptance and realization of unconditional love. Being a child of Chinese immigrant parents and growing up in the hectic surroundings of New York City provided an interesting blend of cultural, belief and family systems. The fact that he realized at a young age that he was gay and felt drawn to acting only made the situation more complex. But he found the courage to face life challenges head-on, immersing himself in yoga and other healing modalities and eventually transforming his life.

Anyone who faces challenging life situations but is committed to finding healing will benefit greatly from this book. By sharing his experiences, perceived by Chong to be "successful" or "a failure" at the time, the author creates a realistic portrayal of a healing path. Learning life lessons is not a straightforward road and often has detours and wrong turns along the way. Within the telling of his story, Chong includes spiritual gems for the reader. A good barometer for a solid spiritual book is this: you can reread it over and over and find new gems each time. *Sage Sapien: From Karma to Dharma* by Johnson Chong is this kind of book—it is to be savored and reread!

—Deborah Lloyd, Reader's Favorite Book Reviews, 5 Stars

Insightful and filled with lessons of self-awareness, self-acceptance, and personal growth, *Sage Sapien: From Karma to Dharma* by Johnson Chong is a compelling and gripping autobiography that follows the journey of a first-generation Asian American gay man torn between the traditional values he's grown up with and the inner freedom that is required to set his life free. Follow the story to learn how he transitioned from a self-loathing individual, shredding his old beliefs, to making choices that allowed him to embrace who he truly is and to forge a personality that aligns with his vision.

One immediately discerns the inner struggle in the protagonist from the insightful opening: "We are told over and over again that we are products of our environment. But I refused to become the apple that fell right under the tree. I never felt like I belonged to my tree, or to the metaphorical apple orchard itself." He talks about his struggles growing up in NYC and the life-changing lessons he learned. There is a powerful dichotomy between the conservative Eastern values of the author's parents and the freedoms of America culture, and the author allows readers to experience his frustrations and emotional turmoil as he struggles to find his own identity.

Sage Sapien: From Karma to Dharma is inspiring, honest, and utterly delightful, and I enjoyed how the author is able to understand himself, doing great inner work that culminates in self-acceptance and freedom. As I read Johnson Chong's story, I began to understand the challenge each of us faces when it comes to choosing who we are against what the world wants us to be. It's a book with wonderful lessons for everyone and I highly recommend it!

—Divine Zape, Reader's Favorite Book Reviews, 5 Stars

Sage Sapien: From Karma to Dharma by Johnson Chong is an insightful book that takes readers into a different dimension as the author unfolds his spiritual journey beginning from his childhood. At a young age, his parents left an inedible mark on his growing up. He speaks about how his parents' influence takes him on a journey of self-evolution. Beginning from his piano lessons to martial arts and history lessons, the author tells readers how he comes to a crossroads trying to comprehend the old regime and the new replacement. His personal journey reflects the collective unconscious patterns where the freedom to be free is denied and how habitual patterns are rooted in the five themes of abuse, abandonment, betrayal, denial, and rejection.

It is a memoir about seeking the truth, exploring spiritual practices like Reiki, meditation, yoga, and finding the purpose of life which is required to untangle everyone from the emotional baggage they carry. It will take readers to another realm where they will feel the need for self-realization and the understanding that nobody owns them. The author's emotional trauma inflicted upon him while growing up, the obstacles and hindrances he faced, and finally breaking free from the old attachments and moving towards self-actualization are empowering and encouraging for readers.

I liked the author's use of the words 'sage sapien'—this gives a radiance to the wisdom and truth everyone seeks during their lifetime and paves the way for humans to reconnect with their bodies and hearts through inner wisdom. It is a good memoir that will make everyone look into their lives and see the damage caused to them through modern consumerism, mass depletion of natural resources, the need for instant gratification, and the rise of mental health problems worldwide. It is a book for all those seeking to discover their inner selves and find their peaceful place where they are not bogged down by rules and principles laid down by others.

—Mamta Madhavan, Reader's Favorite Book Reviews, 5 Stars

Sage Sapien: From Karma to Dharma is an inspirational nonfiction memoir written by Johnson Chong. The author is an international yogi, meditation guide and coach. He's also a public speaker and group leader. Growing up as a gay and rebellious son of deeply conservative Chinese immigrant parents was challenging at best and left him with residual reserves of anger. His mother was a prototypical tiger mom whose expectations, rages and beatings terrorized her kids, and her own mistreatment by her husband made family life a stressful one. While their early years were spent in Brooklyn, where the family owned a small grocery store featuring live fish, they moved to Queens when Chong was 7 years old, and he felt increasingly isolated not only from his family but from the kids in school. College was a long sought-after escape from an untenable situation, but it wasn't until nearly the end of his first year at SUNY Geneseo that the author realized he wanted to go into acting. He won a coveted place at SUNY Purchase where he would continue his studies. Acting was the beginning of a healing process as well as an awakening of his self-awareness.

Johnson Chong's *Sage Sapien: From Karma to Dharma* is a well-written, frank and fearless account of the author's childhood and the paths to knowledge that he's chosen since then. I particularly enjoyed getting to know this engaging author. He's got the ability to make a reader feel as though he's directly communicating with them; as if they were sitting together and casually having a conversation. He's also able to communicate quite effectively, making it easy to see his family home, understand the challenges he faced in acting class, and share in the spiritual journey he embarks upon. His story is profound and inspirational, and it gives the reader insights into life growing up as a gay Asian youth from a conservative background. *Sage Sapien: From Karma to Dharma* is highly recommended.

—Jack Magnus, Reader's Favorite Book Reviews, 5 Stars

Sage Sapien: From Karma to Dharma is a non-fiction memoir about a young Chinese gay man in America and his struggle with the polarizing influences in his life. In this book, Johnson talks about his challenges with reconciling his own sexuality with his parents' preferred view of how they would want things to be, which is a conventional marriage and children. The book is divided into several chapters, each dealing with a specific topic, and each chapter has been titled accordingly which makes it easy to tell at a glance what topic is covered. The book then delves into Johnson's upbringing in a traditional Chinese household in America and being a first-generation Asian American, his sexual orientation as a gay man and what it meant coming out to his parents, how and when he was drawn to spirituality and philosophy, his discovery and continuing practice of yoga and his multiple trips to India to explore more, his other journeys around the world and what he learned, and much more.

Sage Sapien: From Karma to Dharma by Johnson Chong especially focuses on what being gay meant in his life and his ongoing spiritual journey to discover the meaning of life. It is easy to empathize with Johnson when he describes how his parents didn't understand him or accept his sexual orientation. He also writes in detail about what made him interested in exlore meditation, yoga, reiki, and other healing practices. Although the story definitely covers some heavy and serious subjects, Johnson's writing style remains witty, candid, and humorous at times. Hopefully, books like these will help parents understand their children more and accept them as they are. This is a great read!

—Gisela Dixon, Reader's Favorite Book Reviews, 5 Stars

Sage Sapien:
From Karma to Dharma

by Johnson Chong

ISBN 978-1-63393-813-7

Cover Photography: Chad Wagner
Makeup: Derrick Little

Published by

◤ köehlerbooks™

210 60th Street
Virginia Beach, VA 23451
800-435-4811
www.koehlerbooks.com

SAGE SAPIEN

From Karma to Dharma

JOHNSON CHONG

VIRGINIA BEACH
CAPE CHARLES

I dedicate this book to all those who have
ever felt weird, rejected and pressured to conform to a
Truth that is not their own.

And gratitude to my family, friends and teachers
who have loved and challenged me in ways that hurt.
I am the better for it now.

TABLE OF
CONTENTS

CHAPTER 1

PLANTING THE SEEDS: THE BEGINNINGS OF A SPIRITUAL JOURNEY

"I am not what happened to me, I am what I choose to become."

CARL JUNG

We are told over and over again that we are products of our environment. But I refused to become the apple that fell right under the tree. I never felt like I belonged to my tree, or to the metaphorical apple orchard itself. I had a deep wish to transform into a different tree altogether. What if I wanted to become an exotic coconut tree or papaya tree instead, or all of the above?

For as long as I can remember, I yearned to connect to that which was greater than me and my plight. This deep desire to become something more than the product of verbal, emotional and physical abuse was planted in me probably before I was born. But to understand the unfolding of this spiritual journey, the story begins when I was a child.

My parents enrolled me into piano school and martial arts simultaneously when I was ten. I don't know where my parents received the sudden inspiration. Perhaps it was something they read in the Chinese newspaper, or they were feeling competitive when their friends boasted of the extracurricular activities their kids successfully juggled. During this period of my life, my parents started to invest in my holistic wellness, though at the time I was completely unaware of the effects that would ripple into my adult life.

Like any boy at that age, I lashed out and resisted the new activities because they were unfamiliar and felt like a form of punishment. I had a strong disposition to escape into fantasy worlds through TV shows that my parents strictly regulated. The living room was routinely put under lock and key until we finished our homework, or when my mother decided we didn't deserve TV time. I saw this parental dictatorship as a ruthless impingement on my free will. Nowadays, at dinner, I see young parents thrusting tablets and gadgets in front of their kids to distract them so they can take a breather from parenting for a minute. My parents were the complete opposite. They policed everything we did. They wanted to make sure we were becoming the brightest and most well-rounded individuals.

Needless to say, I had no say in piano lessons. I had a love-hate relationship with the piano. It was difficult at first to sit still and practice for what seemed like an eternity. The repetition frustrated my drive to constantly move. To sit in front of the piano and home laser-like focus onto the music felt like what I imagined it would be like to wear a straitjacket as a mental patient. I was consumed by frustration when I could not get the scales or musical phrases after numerous attempts. I would scream, throw tantrums and occasionally fling the sheet music across the room. With practice and time, learning Mozart, Bach, Beethoven, Brahms and all the classics calmed and connected me to my inward grace, which was reflected outward through musicality. The piano taught me to focus, concentrate and coordinate. These repetitive scales and drills were my first forays into a state of concentration, which became a precursor for meditation later on in life.

My hate for the piano stemmed from ten years of rebelling against authority. I had an unwavering disgust for authority and took every opportunity to do what I was told not to do. So, when I decided to go on strike and not practice, my mother would whoop my butt, to put it lightly. Not only was I wasting good money by not practicing, but also, apparently, if I didn't do everything according to her vision, I would devolve into a degenerate good-for-nothing. It was oppressive. This relationship of love-hate went on for eight more years until I moved on from it. And the piano, in the end, mirrored a more profound pattern in my relationship with my mother, to be realized later.

Martial arts was also thrust upon me. My older brother was getting picked on in school, and my father decided it was time to build character through self-defense. Like everything my parents ever did in life, they didn't ask. They made an executive decision and I found myself in a kung fu class without much explanation. I met the start of my budding relationship with kung fu with a familiar hesitation that came from feeling unacknowledged. Eventually, my fascination and adoration of Greek mythology and the TV shows *Hercules* and *Xena: Warrior Princess* convinced me to enjoy this new role as a warrior. My father invited a master of Wing Chun to the house twice a week. We were studying the martial arts system Bruce Lee studied. When I eventually bought into the whole thing, within a few weeks I expected to fight off an entire horde of baddies like in *Enter the Dragon*. Sifu put my expectations in check. Boy was I way off the mark.

For six months, it was grueling work. We had to do knuckle push-ups on only our ring finger and little finger knuckles. The point was to flatten the knuckles, calcify the bones, in order to increase the power of our punches. Then there were the forms we had to learn. I only got up to the first form and was never allowed to progress because I didn't put in enough practice time and hence did not show improvement. My brother, on the other hand, was motivated to stand up for himself at school, and as a result progressed much faster than I did. I grew frustrated, and was envious of his progress, but blamed everyone else for getting in the way of my advancement.

After six months of being at a standstill, our old sifu had health complications and we were enrolled into a Shaolin kung fu school with Master Gao in Flushing, Queens. He was one of the fight choreographers of *Crouching Tiger Hidden Dragon*. We practiced downstairs in the basement of his KTV bar. Karaoke by night, kung fu by day. It was strange, but I didn't know any better, and Master Gao didn't seem to care what people thought, so I thought it was normal.

At eleven, through Shaolin, I discovered how to dance. I really enjoyed practicing the forms. They were more fluid than Wing Chun. I felt strong yet supple when embodying the energies of the tiger, the crane, the snake and the dragon. According to the *Secret Language of Birthdays* by Gary Goldschneider and Joost Elffers, I was born during "the week of dreamers and dancers." No wonder I felt right at home with the Shaolin style.

If you wanted to knock out eight bad guys who had you cornered in a dark alleyway, Wing Chun was the way to do it. The less showy movements of Wing Chun were functional and direct, while the Shaolin kung fu forms evoked a sense of beauty and grace that felt like a celebration of nature through dance. With all of my anger toward everyone around me, my parents, my siblings and other kids at school, I should have wanted to knock everyone out, but all I wanted to do was dance. Shaolin taught me how to control my breath and create internal heat and energy. It enlivened me physically. Emotionally, I felt calmer, mentally focused. Even though I was a loner until the age of fourteen and never made any long-lasting friends, I felt undefeatable and found solace in my loneliness.

And so, through the unexpected influence of my parents, I was well on my way toward a journey of self-evolution. The piano opened my heart to patience and discipline, while martial arts centered me physically and energetically.

Nutritionally, my mother brought home all types of bizarre herbal tonics and tinctures from the traditional Chinese apothecary: bitter roots and barks of trees brewed into a tonic; beetle soup; cow brain soup; fungus this, that or the other. Was it divine intervention instructing my mother to brew her concoctions to purify my spirit? This was the same mother who, later, when I told her that I was gay at the age of twenty-six, went to the Chinese herbalist in search for a cure to save her son. My mother was definitely a witchy herbalist in another life. Her intentions were always based on love, but her love was clouded by the emotional traumas of her upbringing, and, unfortunately, her love often expressed itself in outbursts and violent actions.

One day she brought home a woman who taught qigong. I was not wearing glasses at the time, but my vision was progressively getting worse, probably due to staring at the television screen for too long and burying my face into textbooks and piano scores. I don't know why some children developed nearsightedness from the beginning and why my vision was fine until I turned ten years old. I secretly want to blame puberty and the genetically modified food of the nineties.

Mrs. Wu, a peculiar woman with a short bob of curly white hair, entered my living room one evening. "Surprise! Here's another investment for your wellbeing! Courtesy of your mother." *Oh great, what has she in store for me now?* I thought. I didn't mind Mrs. Wu, actually. At that age, I assumed all Asian women to be screechy, loud, ferocious and forceful like my mother, but Mrs. Wu offered a kinder and softer contrast. My mother watched her like a hawk and backseat drove the whole time. Mrs. Wu spoke when she needed to speak and focused on teaching me a meditation technique similar to the yogic concentration technique, which I learned much later called *tratak*. I trusted her quite easily and enjoyed her teaching me meditation. I thought, *Hey lady, you earned my respect. I never met anyone who made my mother quiet for so long.* It must have been the mystical essence that she carried about her.

She came weekly for a number of sessions to manipulate the energies around my frontal lobe and the back of my skull. She had me stare at a stick of curly fortune bamboo. I was instructed to stare at the bamboo for thirty minutes every day without blinking, to the point that tears streamed down my face. The point was to purify the pathways in my eyes. The toxins were said to leave through the tear ducts. I took her at her word but was undisciplined when it came to practicing.

Soon she stopped coming. I don't remember why. Maybe my mother grew impatient at the results. I still had to wear glasses in the end, but my vision stopped getting worse, so that was a plus. As peculiar as it may sound for an eleven-year-old, I did enjoy the sensation of staring into the bamboo. It felt like I was being absorbed inside myself. All my problems at home and school disappeared into the background, and I just felt the pulsation of my heart and the heat in my hands. There was a palpable buzz of energy around my skull, and I found a few moments' peace within.

With the juxtaposition of investing in my wellbeing and hurting me, my mother is by far the most contradictory and complex person in my life. I spent many hours contemplating why she behaved the way she did. I imagined logical motivations for her verbal and physical aggressions when she exploded. Even though I empathized with her life struggles and intellectualized her raison d'être, I still wasn't emotionally able to process her furious outbursts and my father's indifferent attitude about everything.

She was like Doctor Manette from *A Tale of Two Cities*, who was imprisoned by the French aristocracy. Every American junior high schooler was forced to analyze this Charles Dickens classic in English literature. It was probably the government's way of making sure the younger generation cultivated a healthy American attitude toward the working class and democracy.

In the book, society at large was in this bestial "eye for an eye" mode, out for justice and vengeance with little regard for who was hurt along the way. I couldn't help but picture my parents suffering the same way when they were persecuted by the communists for being born into a family of landowners. My father spent most of his twenties in jail during the Cultural Revolution in the 1960s.

Throughout my childhood, whether I was by myself or in the company of my brother and sister, I caught glimpses of my parents' history. When my behavior challenged my parents' patience, they got nostalgic until their defenses went back up again. My father didn't know how to express his frustrations at being the family provider in a country he wouldn't have been in if it weren't for the communists. He let out his frustrations by beating my mother. I spent many nights processing how these communists that I was learning about in school messed my parents up, and now they were taking it out on me. I didn't know when or how these emotional outbursts would arrive, so I was always on guard when I was around them, fearing that I would be the object of their letting off steam.

The struggle between the French aristocracy and the peasant class, though the time, place and circumstances differed, struck a resonant chord in me. Reading Dickens' story, I pictured my parents going through the universal themes of denial, abuse, betrayal, abandonment and rejection. Just like the French peasantry felt wronged by the aristocracy and sought vengeance through violence, my parents were the objects of revenge and labeled as enemies of the state.

With every history lesson involving a struggle between an old regime and the new replacement, I found myself at the crossroads, weighing the pros and cons between the two sides. Why couldn't everyone just get along? Then the younger generation would not mirror the footsteps of this endless cycle of pain and suffering. I was a naïve idealist with romantic notions, undeniably driven by the poetic nature of my Piscean soul.

Little did I know, I was not alone in sharing the themes of *A Tale of Two Cities*. This collective unconscious patterning of being denied the right to feel like a free human being is as real as the pollution in the air we breathe. Whether you feel abused, betrayed, abandoned and rejected by your own family, friends, countrymen or country is beside the point. The personal story is interwoven with the collective tapestry—micro to macro. The unconscious person seems to function with a parroting mechanism that sequesters them in a prison of conformity. "If everyone else is doing it, then I'll just blindly follow for convenience sake." The lazy man's guide to life is actually based in the fear of sticking out like a sore thumb. So how could I get mad at my parents for everything they put me through if I could chalk it up to their defense mechanisms? Shouldn't I blame it on social and environmental conditioning instead?

When I was fourteen, I opened up in a big way to the first real friend I could trust. My childhood-best-friend phase happened much later than most because I was so afraid of being rejected the way my parents were rejected by the country they were born in. Joanna was the first person I came out to, besides my brother and sister. My siblings' support seemed to come by default when I told them. Because we shared similar struggles being born to our parents, their acceptance of my gayness was offered almost in a spirit of commiseration rather than in acknowledgment. Telling Joanna was a huge step for me in trusting another person who didn't share my plight and who could potentially reject me.

I realized that everyone, whether in larger or smaller doses, had experienced these qualities of suffering, and that all suffering and unconscious habitual patterns were rooted in these five themes of denial, abuse, betrayal, abandonment and rejection. Each one bled into the other and the distinctions between them were hard to pinpoint.

And so the seeds of my holistic journey were planted at a young age by the same people who unconsciously worked to spoil the fruits of the tree. It was ironic how the same parents who wanted so badly for me to become the best version of myself were the biggest donors to my mental, emotional and physical abuse.

It is now and only now, after a culmination of several life-changing events, that I am able to appreciate these dark lessons of my childhood. My parents spent most of their free time micromanaging every facet of my life from how I ate, what I ate, what I studied, how I spent my free time, what career I should explore, etc. The list multiplied like an unwanted weed in the garden. And my rebellious nature only worsened their fight to control my destiny. Inside, my true self was shrouded under an army of those thorny weeds. I wasn't ready to detach from my suffering, but if I could give my younger self one piece of advice, I would tell him, "Remember that you can feel the sun on your face anytime you want if only you would choose to hack away at the overgrowth of unwanted weeds."

As a teenager, I didn't think I had a choice but to resign in silent obedience. I know now that we always have a choice.

🪷

It is with this spirit that I explored how the spiritual practices I came across, like yoga, meditation, bodywork, Reiki and shamanic-inspired practices, helped me evolve into a productive modern man, making my way through the age of a declining heterosexist and patriarchal paradigm. And it is with this spirit that I share with you how I integrate ancient wisdom to turn away my unwanted guests— stress and anxiety—when they come knocking at my door.

The first piece of advice that I can share is that the weeds will never stop growing. They will keep infesting your garden—like destructive gossip, wars, and atrocious acts of human defilement. Whatever notions of paradise or perfection you may have that stem from the Garden of Eden or its parallel should be tossed out the window. Complaining about the weeds doesn't do us any good. We spend so much time complaining and critiquing ourselves and others instead of savoring the challenge of finding a solution. The challenge lies in moving from indecision to taking action. We really only have two simple choices in life: Get down and dirty and remember to trim the overgrowth from time to time, or let a jungle of laziness and ignorance enshroud us.

Unless you were born a saint or an avatar without lifetimes of earthly karma to work out, you are just like me. I don't care if you are straight, gay, a man, a woman, black, white or other. The sooner we realize that the purpose of life is to help each other untangle from the proverbial emotional luggage we came in with, the happier we will be. Some of us arrived here with a Louis Vuitton bag of crap, and others a plastic bag full of crap. But at the end of the day, we all breathe, eat, drink and excrete the same self-sabotaging thoughts. It is how we perceive this game we are in, and what we choose to do with it, that makes us or breaks us. In the words of Carl Jung, "I am not what happened to me, I am what I choose to become."

CHAPTER 2

DISTINGUISHING BETWEEN PAIN AND SUFFERING

ॐ

"Pain is what the world does to you.
Suffering is what you do to yourself."

BUDDHA

Distinguishing the difference between pain and suffering was pivotal in my journey to becoming whole, and we all learn the difference in one way or another. For me, it came from marking my body. To truly discover myself, I had to take physical action to heal from the disconnectedness I felt in my childhood.

For the majority of my adolescence and early adulthood, I chalked up a lot of my internalized hurt and pain as normal. I swept it under the carpet and hoped that no one would discover my suppressive tendencies. I have a distinct memory of my mother tying me to the high chair at the age of three and leaving me in the hallway of our fourth-floor Brooklyn apartment. She was trying to teach me a lesson. It was either to discipline me because I wasn't eating something she thought would be good for me, or I was playing with my food and making a mess. Maybe it was both; I don't remember. What I do remember is the feeling of being in an ivory tower, chained up, and forced to do something against my will. I was forced to resist my natural state of play.

This is one of the first childhood memories I have when I'm prompted to recall my youth. Most of the marker points into my past are based in emotional trauma. Growing up with the shadows of my parents' own traumas, I constantly feared suffering the wrath of an angry mother, a disappointed father, or both.

After a good beating, I often found myself in a state of confusion. When the tantrums and the crying subsided, I suppressed the experience in order to deny that my mother had hurt me so. *How could this woman who is supposed to love and protect me hit me with such force? Well, she said it was to make me better, so perhaps there was something wrong with my actions and I was at fault.* The human brain is designed to protect us from danger, and our bodies are even more resilient, so it was natural for my young brain to rationalize it all. It was the only way to make sense of the world.

Being left outside screaming and kicking, tied to a high chair for what seemed like an eternity, engrained patterns that would affect the way I made decisions for a long time to come. The three-year-old me was forced into physical submission and carried the fear of betrayal, abandonment, and rejection well into my adult relationships.

When the rage settled, and the beating stopped, my mother would explain her reason for beating me. The unruliness of a wild child was simply not allowed. I was being punished for being myself, so the logical inference was that I was not a good person. Something must have been fundamentally wrong with me. Over the years, I conditioned myself to think that my very essence was the cause of my many beatings, and therefore the root cause of my suffering.

With my current understanding of pain versus suffering, I clearly understand what the Buddha meant when he explained that pain is the physical sensation that happens to us, and suffering is the attachment to the stories behind the sensation. Suffering was caused by my inability to let go of the pain and my tendency to identify with all the titles that pain bestowed on me.

There were many secret benefits to playing the victim and the wounded child. Carrying a scar felt like a badge of honor, putting me in the ranks of the ancient Greek heroes, like Hercules, who also suffered greatly because of his parents' flaws. Warped as it may be, suffering was a way of getting recognition and validation that I existed, even if it meant identifying with being the abused. It was comfortable to stay in the role that was known to me.

Part of the work I do is grounded in physicality—movement of the muscles, the bones and the connective tissue. From this perspective, it's very evident that pain is a sensation and suffering is created when the edges of comfort and pleasure are challenged. I witness it in my private sessions when novice movers complain of pain. Oftentimes, the pain comes from a stretch that they are not accustomed to, and as a result they create some story around how they cannot do it. The key to evolving on the spiritual path is discerning when actual pain is trying to keep us safe and when we're creating stories of resistance around pain, which lead to our inevitable suffering.

For example, a couple of years ago, I decided to get another tattoo.

My first one was at seventeen. It was illegal for minors to get tattoos without parental consent, so I was adamant about getting inked in defiance of authority and my parents. With steadfast conviction, I got a fake ID from where all the NYU kids were getting them and marched to Greenwich Village with my most trusted friend at the time, Joanna. I convinced myself that it was a necessary act of coolness to tattoo my zodiac sign on my navel.

It would be my rite of passage, marking my emancipation into adulthood: two Piscean fish swirling around the point where life begins. I was redefining my relationship with my mother by reclaiming my navel. I stood firm in this symbolic act of severing the umbilical cord between me and my mother.

I thought I would never get another tattoo in my life. The navel is one of the most sensitive regions on the body. I left the tattoo parlor bandaged in plastic, and as I made my way home on the subway, my body involuntarily quivered like the legs of an abused dog.

So when I had a dream of getting Metatron's cube of life tattooed on my forearm, I shuddered at the thought of going through it all again. But this time around, sitting on the chair, I experienced a very clear distinction between pain and suffering. At first, I writhed in pain, making all types of strange sounds and faces to distract myself from feeling the needle on the sensitive curves of my forearm and wrist. It was a failed attempt to avoid feeling the obvious sensation of pain. I suffered for five hours due to my aversion to discomfort and my attachment to comfort.

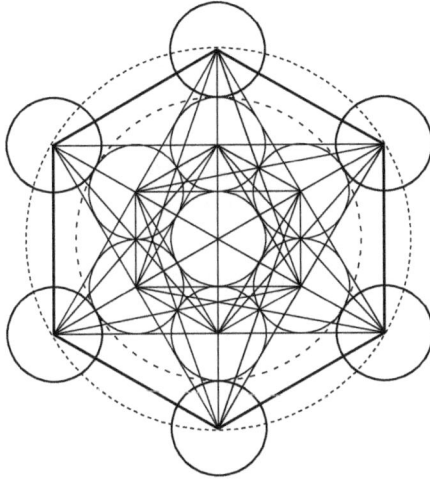

Fig 1. Metatron is the angelic form of the Prophet and is mentioned briefly in the Talmud and old Jewish mystic texts. He is the celestial scribe and God's right-hand man who recorded the word of God. There are many theories around the meaning of the cube of life. This sacred geometrical symbol isn't to be understood through the logical mind. To me, at one point, the thirteen circles represented each of the thirteen archangels, and at other points in time, thirteen was the thirteen steps toward enlightenment as seen in the stupas built in Nepal. Now, I see the shapes not as belonging to any one particular lineage but as an amalgamation of universal truths compressed into sacred art. This symbol transmits to me a feeling of wholeness and connection to the universe, not to be understood with the logical mind, but rather felt with everything else.

The artist said it would take about two hours prior to starting, but he took an hour's worth of smoke breaks in between. For him, it was necessary to smoke two to three cigarettes during each break to get his symmetry on point. I simply couldn't bear it anymore, and something had to change. During the last two hours, instead of squirming away from the pain, I zoomed into it like a scientist with a microscope. I closed my eyes and followed the needle instead. I observed each prick and scrape of my flesh from a different perspective. It took a considerable amount of focus and concentration to un-attach from the pain.

I say un-attach versus detach. Detaching would be avoiding the sensations altogether, like drugging myself up on painkillers and passing out during the entire process. Un-attaching was a conscious decision to own the pain without generating a story of suffering around it.

I entered a trance for the last two hours. The experience felt similar to occasions when I spent quality time doing something I loved or hanging around people I loved. Normally when I experience something excruciatingly laborious and tedious, time expands. During the last two hours, time felt like it was expanding and contracting all at once. It was timelessness. I entered the parlor in broad daylight, and I left in the dark of night. All the screaming and writhing around was suffering that I created because I was trying my damnedest to escape experiencing the raw sensation of burning flesh. And somewhere along the way, when I couldn't take it anymore, there was a shift and a new understanding. The entire experience was such an appropriate metaphor for how I dealt with most situations in my life. And the addition of my new tattoo marked also a new shift into the incredible power of choice that I have.

We all share this conditioned defense mechanism that we need to challenge constantly in order to break out of our small-mindedness. Buddhism centralizes its entire philosophy around the notion that if we are to end our suffering, we must embrace pain as an essential part of life. Knowing that everyone shares these same themes of pain and suffering, and that the point of life is to renegotiate the terms in which we choose to hold or not hold onto the pain. I am currently in a place where I choose to move through life less seriously on a daily basis.

CHAPTER 3

DRAMA IN
DRAMA SCHOOL

"All the world's a stage, and all the men and women merely players."

WILLIAM SHAKESPEARE

I discovered late in acting school, at nineteen, with my speech teacher, Leigh Dillon, that I was projecting my childhood issues of not being good enough into her class. I got frustrated when she made us do tip-of-the-tongue exercises with wine corks in our mouths. The objective was to make our sibilants less thick and lispy, something that I was overly self-conscious of as a gay teenager. Overly sibilant gay kids always got made fun of and bullied. I was always weird and tall for my age, so people left me alone, and I floated by in a self-contained bubble all the way through high school with very few close friends. Though I appeared self-sufficient and not needing the closeness of other people, I was hyper aware of how sibilant my *S*s were because I wanted to control how others perceived me. I didn't want immediate assumptions made of me.

Speech class was all about neutralizing our speech patterns. Some of my classmates had to get rid of their Midwest-isms or Southern drawls, while I had to stop my irregular choices of broad New York vowel changes. As a second-generation Asian American growing up in a very Jewish, Latino and Jamaican area of Midwood in Brooklyn until the age of seven, then moving to Woodhaven in Queens where there was an added Slavic, Eastern European influence, it was no wonder I was a late bloomer when it came to speaking.

I spoke Chinese with my parents at home, watched PBS for English lessons with the British lady, and instead of daycare, my father found it convenient to leave me all day in a kitchen of Rastafarian cooks. He would occasionally do this so he could finish his delivery routes. I was that Asian kid whose parents had a Chinese fish market and sold funny smelling Chinese groceries. Sometimes I would say tomato the British way and greet my mom "Hey mon" like a mini Bob Marley.

When we were told to decondition our speech, I realized that I had unconsciously picked up vowel changes from different ethnic groups. My cousins sounded like they were clearly from Brooklyn, and here I was in speech class feeling like an anomaly because I didn't have strong New York-isms to neutralize, just weird Johnson-isms to figure out.

During this deconditioning process, I felt singled out. Speech class re-highlighted that my peculiar habits were picked up to protect myself from pain. We were made aware of how we chose our speech patterns and were graded on "correcting" it, even though Leigh explained that it didn't mean we would just delete our speech patterns, never to be used again. The purpose was to expand our horizons and our range as actors. Sure, some actors like Al Pacino or Christopher Walken have their signature vocal expressions and are very successful at it. However, acting school was all about adding more colors into our crayon box. Still, I felt like I was under attack.

While getting graded on our Mid-Atlantic received pronunciation of our Shakespearean monologue—Rumour's prologue from *Henry IV*, Part II—I cringed at hearing the playback on my voice recorder.

This was a full-on frontal assault of Johnson's Fortress of Comfort. *Why do I even need to neutralize my Ss?* To the four gay actors in my class, me included, our acting teachers, without directly saying it, essentially said, "You would be limiting the roles you could play" if the problem weren't rectified. In my head, that reinforced the fact that I was about to enter a profession where appearing gay would work against me. Not only was I a minority with less substantial roles to audition for, but I was a gay minority who would have even less of a chance. My self-saboteur was fully active, chopping away at my confidence, telling me I didn't deserve any kind of success because being gay was bad—another aspect of the good-versus-bad approval programming from Mommy and Daddy that I couldn't seem to overwrite.

I had a massive fear program embedded deep in my computer processor with the root file originating in fear of my mother's rejection for not being good enough. At fifteen, I caught the broom my mother hurled at me and pulled it out of her hand, and that was last she ever tried to physically punish me. But the imprint had been left, and I still sought the approval of motherly figures in my life and hoped but never believed that I would be accepted as a good son. This duplicated itself like a virus, and I created the same perverse relationship with all my female teachers. I couldn't accept that they were actually on my side.

Leigh was meticulous at her job. She had coached stars like Denzel Washington, Naomi Watts, Liev Schreiber and Julianne Moore. And here I was, freaking out, thinking that she was out to hurt me in the middle of the classroom if I didn't pronounce words correctly. In retrospect, my internal dialogue was rather insane.

At the end of the year, we had evaluations and private meetings with our teachers to assess our progress. That was always a minefield in acting school with me because it wasn't like in high school where you got an A or an F on a chemistry test. We were being graded on our intangible progress as actors—as human beings! These meetings always amplified the anxiety levels of my entire class. We started as a small group of twenty-two aspiring actors, and each year some people chose to leave, while others were dismissed from the program. In the end, we graduated with fifteen. I was on the chopping block for two of the four years that I was there. This happened because I was constantly comparing myself to my classmates and shooting myself in the foot before I even gave myself a chance. On one hand, I was actually excited each day to learn about what made me tick. It was like being in a dissection lab for my psyche. On the other hand, my first-year acting teacher, Dale Moffit, told us that acting school was not therapy. So, even though exploration was encouraged, there was still pressure to deliver.

During my end-of-the-semester evaluations with Leigh, she reaffirmed very simply, "You are enough. You are enough." I tried to hush the tears welling up until I left the room. It was the kind of raw, authentic emotion that I wanted to show through my performances but, ironically, only came when I was dealing with my own crap.

That was my breakthrough moment. I realized that to "shine" meant getting rid of all the baggage that I had been carrying for so long. I was enough. I didn't need all the extra layers that prevented my realness and true essence from expressing itself to the world. I didn't need to hide behind a mask anymore.

This was the consistent feedback I got from every teacher: "Who is Johnson? Where is the truth behind what you're doing?" *How the hell am I supposed to know?* I thought. This was the first time in my life that I was being asked these questions. Every day of acting school involved me having to untangle myself from this big ball of confusion in order to pacify a ticking time bomb that could sloppily explode into a million pieces.

There was one major incident where acting crossed the line into therapy during my sophomore year. It put me into a spiral of depression that led me to smoking cigarettes and drinking more than I should have. The actors from the other years always hosted parties after their shows where all the actors in the program would be invited. People would hide alcohol from me because I would lose control and some unprepared soul would have to console me and eventually drag me out of the bathroom. At many a party, I could be found either blurting out stories of why I was so messed up or wallowing in my misery behind the bathtub curtain with a bottle of vodka in hand. It seemed like I was channeling all the characters out of a bleak Russian play about existential angst.

Well, it made sense. We were studying Anton Chekhov sophomore year with John Gould Rubin in scene study class. During our final scene study presentation, I opted to do three back-to-back scenes from *Ivanov*. The requirement was to present only one scene, two max, since our class was an odd number of people. I knew I was on the verge of getting the boot, so I openly chose to do all the scenes of act three—the climax of the play where Ivanov's reality flips upside down, and he is sent into a fit of despair.

Long story short: Ivanov was this melancholic character drowning in debt in a miserably repressed Russian town. He married a Jew, Anna, for her dowry, but never got it because her parents disowned her for converting. She also happened to be dying of tuberculosis. He got into a situation where he started to develop feelings for his creditor's twenty-year-old daughter Sasha.

In act three, all the external and internal pressures are ripe to erupt as Ivanov deals with all of these people simultaneously. First, his debt collector's husband, Lebedev, begs Ivanov to repay the loan to his wife, even offering a secret loan. Shortly after, his wife's doctor rips Ivanov to pieces for cheating on Anna. Then he's caught in a whirlwind of mixed emotions when Sasha addresses their relationship. All of this climaxes when Anna angrily confronts Ivanov about his infidelity and rebukes him for marrying her only for her money and destroying her life. Amid all the guilt, shame, self-loathing and depression, Ivanov becomes enraged and insults her with hateful words. Since she doesn't know about the advancement of her condition, Ivanov scornfully calls out the doctor's prognosis of Anna's impending death. As soon as the hateful words come out of his mouth, he realizes how awful he has been and tries to apologize. He is overcome with emotion and has a meltdown, reprimanding himself on how awful a human being he is.

In scene study, we studied and applied the Stanislavsky method of acting, which focuses on using the imagination and the "magic if." It was all about consciously using the imagination to create the psychological motivations of the character. It involved a lot of script analysis and rehearsing playable objectives with my scene partners. Our focus was not to force an emotional response. If we played the objectives and stayed true to the circumstances, the emotionality of the scene would ring true; otherwise, it would read as disingenuous.

Act three was a long continuous scene that was probably thirty minutes with some text edits. My three different scene partners and I booked slots in the rehearsal room depending on our schedules. Before my final presentation, I had never done the entire act continuously. The back-to-back confrontations with each character opened up the bridge between Ivanov and myself. My psychological issues and his psychological issues merged into each other. His meltdown became my meltdown.

Though the details of our circumstances were not identical, the universality of guilt, shame, depression, self-loathing, fear and anger were undeniably shared between us. When the scene ended, as the actor I should have been able to come back as Johnson. On that day, I could not control my body. I fell to the ground, curled up in a fetal position and fell into a fit of uncontrollable sobbing. Being on another probationary term under the threat of being cut from the program, I buckled under the pressure and lost it completely. Mucous streamed from my nostrils and my stomach convulsed as if I were going to vomit. At that moment, the loathing that Ivanov felt for himself and the loathing I felt for myself were one and the same. The class went silent, and my acting teacher told my scene partner to step away from me. He came over to me and very slowly started the process of bringing me back to the room.

We took a break, and John Gould Rubin told us that our jobs as actors were to create a clear division between ourselves and our characters, and that it was not healthy to blur the lines. What could I do? I shunned the idea of going to the therapist's office. I recalled my experience with one of the school's counselors freshman year. She sat there silently probing me with her eyes while saying things like, "Tell me why you are here." "What do you think could have caused what happened in class?" "Who told you that you were not enough?" "Would you like to share something from your childhood?"

Like Hansel and Gretel, she used breadcrumbs to lure me into my past. Soon enough, I went into verbal diarrhea about my mother. But I thought I had worked it all out in my head, so why was all of this coming out again, and why was I telling this woman didn't know?

From the age of fifteen to eighteen, I started to feel more included by society. Part of it was knowing college was around the corner. That meant freedom from the stifling grasp of my parents. During that time, my parents were having financial tension, causing them to bicker and argue often. And when my father hit my mother or pushed her buttons, she would storm around the apartment and throw a fit until she crumbled into an undone adult-child. In these tender moments, a light would shine through, into the mystery of her past. I understood then why she behaved the way she did.

Her father died when she was young. Her mother basically

abandoned her, leaving her to be raised by her older siblings and relatives. She wasn't able to go to school past the third grade due to worsening social conditions under the budding communist regime. She never learned how to deal with her abandonment issues and took it out on me and my siblings. To survive, she had to toughen up fast. Once, she encountered a psychic in another village who had the reputation of accurately reading someone's future by looking at the lines of their face. These types of practices were deemed dangerous by the Communist Party of China, and it was very dangerous to seek out such people. My mother managed to travel to this other village under the guise of visiting a relative, to receive a reading with this psychic. He had a large head and ill-proportioned legs. He was born disabled with an irregular frame. He told her that she would fly on an airplane to the other side of the world and start a new life. That she was poor now but would not be for the rest of her life. She would have two boys and a girl. Everything she did in life would not come easy. And she would be always the black sheep of the family and should not depend on any of her siblings to help her. She had to rely on her own strength to make it through on her own.

My mother went on to have two sons and a girl, and resourcefully received asylum into the United States. She flew across the Pacific, got her green card and eventually became an American citizen. The American dream achieved. But what a damning prophecy to tell my mother that she would have to be strong and make it on her own. Or perhaps that was her interpretation of the seer's message. My mother always distrusted our relatives on her side of the family, saying that they were always gossiping about her behind her back. She was full of paranoia. It explained so much about her personality. Always frantic and on edge about every little thing she could not control. So, she put the control on what she thought she could control: the three lives that sprang from her womb.

As chaotic as my childhood was with my mother trying to backseat drive my life, in the long run, I developed a new sense of appreciation for our relationship. Subsequently, I thought that I had completely forgiven her and let go of the hell she put me through. But I had only swept everything under the carpet. And it was only natural that my volcano erupted the way it did during my Ivanov scene presentation. Now, it was my mission to become more present and aware of the demons that were hiding under my bed, to know them and understand them so that I would not ever melt down so ungracefully like that ever again.

CHAPTER 4

YOGA TO THE RESCUE

ॐ

"Yoga is the journey of the self, through the self, to the self."

BHAGAVAD GITA

After that initial therapy session, I was put off of therapy until it came knocking on my door again after college. The entire experience frightened me. I emptied the counselor's box of tissues. And though I felt a relief from crying my eyes out, I left the session feeling like I had more issues with no actual solutions. With her minimalist cuing, she masterfully steered me into unearthing things that I didn't consciously know I was still concealing. But it seemed that I couldn't put the lid on my Pandora's box. It was what my teacher John Gould Rubin called emotional masturbation.

Emotional masturbation is exactly as it sounds—getting off on our puddles of grief and despair. As impressive as it is when we see actors emote on stage or on film, we lose interest in the story if the words are muffled by the messiness of raw emotion. We lose interest when we can no longer relate to the story. And that is what I felt like. In my already vulnerable state, I felt like my therapist guided me to another dark room in my soul, where I proceeded to dig myself deeper and deeper into a never-ending pit of sorrow. And for some reason, some part of me enjoyed it.

I left her office full of questions. I walked under the oppressive walkways back to the acting building for rehearsal. These walkways were designed to shield us from the rain and snow, but their hideous façade only amplified the air of depression. The story goes that Purchase College was designed with just the basics so that the artists could create something beautiful on campus. A frugal budget decision if you ask me. When I was there, campus felt like a prison. Even eating felt like prison. With food served in a mess hall overseen by railed encirclements above us, it very much felt like we were inmates being watched by Big Brother.

I was surrounded by melancholy. From the drab, miserable gray skies to the grim brown buildings to the hateful thoughts pounding in my head. Just when I thought I didn't have any more tears, the memories summoned from my therapy session sent me into another massive outbreak of hideous crying. I hid in the basement bathroom of the dance building to avoid being seen. The last time I hated myself that badly was in junior high school. Many people say they have suicidal thoughts in high school. But for me high school was where I learned how to be the lone wolf, and it was a place where people respected my intelligence and kept their distance from me. Also, I knew I was one step closer to leaving the bounds of my parents' expectations.

Junior high was when I felt the most isolated. Those were the years where my mother's actions left long-lasting imprints on my human development. And it was therapy that brought me back to ten years old.

I always knew I was different when I was a child. At the age of four, whenever *Days of Our Lives* came on the TV, I imitated the soap vixens as they lustfully kissed their hunky lovers. So, at ten, it was a big deal to finally come out to my brother and sister. My brother is only a year older than me, and my sister is almost four years younger than me. We didn't always get along, and fought like savages, but something inside of me was dying to express itself.

My coming out to my siblings was not as climactic as I had thought it would be. I was so relieved and pleasantly surprised when my big brother nonchalantly said, "I know. I don't really care." As indifferent as it came out, it was still a pledge of support. My sister didn't know any better and grew up with my secret.

Alien is the best way to describe how I felt. With no exposure to the full meaning of homosexuality, I still knew deep down there was no way my parents would ever approve. Nor would I even dare to bring it up. It's not like I had a real-life counselor in the corner whispering in my ear telling me not to come out to my parents. My intuition told me to hide it from them with all my might. It was an instinct to protect myself.

That's when the proverbial shit splattered all over the fan. My parents never threw anything away—I suppose coming out of a bleak communist regime would make anyone a hoarder—so I figured I'd hide my scrapbook of magazine cutouts of male models in the closet between the layers of never-used blankets. But on that unforeseen day, I came home to my mother cleaning in her anally retentive way of taking things out and refolding them. I found her flipping through the pages. The Calvin Klein underwear models and the various other half-naked male models were particularly alarming to her.

She turned into a banshee. Screaming at the top of her lungs, demanding to know who it belonged to. She equated the cutouts with pornography. After screaming at my defenseless six-year-old sister who did not have the courage at that young age to cover for me, the finger was pointed at me. I was accused of being a pervert. She demanded to know what kind of things I was learning in *American* school. "Why are we working so hard to send you to school to make you into a pervert?" She couldn't even bring herself to say gay, or homosexual. But, I always knew that *pervert* was synonymous with *gay* in her book. She was so livid that the only way she could express herself was through brute force. Friends of mine from the South told me stories of their parents forcing them to select which switch they wanted to get beat with. I had no such luck in selecting my form of punishment. My mother went straight for the leather belt. She chased me around the house whipping me until I finally gave up, huddled into a little ball under the sofa. I knew it was the only way to get her to stop—fall into submission. I had to wait out the storm. When the storm was over, she quickly left the scene, carefully avoiding showing any signs of sadness or remorse in front of us.

I was used to the physical explosions from her. It was what she did afterward that sent me into an emotional lockdown throughout junior high school. Two days later, she showed up at my school and took me out of my fifth-grade class. It was so embarrassing. She had another Chinese woman with her who acted as her translator. I thought it was all over, but she dragged me down to the guidance counselor's office, and that was when the interrogation began. I understood exactly what my mother was saying in Cantonese to her friend and what the counselor was saying to the translator. The translator was on my mother's side, and I sensed that she shared her conservative views. I saw the two of them as the same, and I wanted the guidance counselor to take me into her arms and shield me, but I knew I had to keep my poker face on.

My mother took out of her bag the black-and-white marble notebook that I had turned into a male underwear model scrapbook and slammed it on the table. She then started yelling at the counselor in Cantonese.

"What kind of perverted things are you teaching my child in school here. My child is supposed to be getting an education!" It was belligerent and crass, very much consistent with my mother's rough-and-tumble way. There were three different voices asking me why I created the scrapbook: my mother on the one hand conjecturing that I was molested by a male teacher, the translator trying to find words to phrase my mother's concerns, and the guidance counselor looking at me with great concern, knowing that I was in the roughest of spots.

I folded my arms and shoved my hands deeply into my armpits, dropping my chin to my chest, head toward the counselor, in an attempt to avoid eye contact with my mother. My answer to every question was "No" or "I don't know." I was so intimidated I couldn't even make up a story about how some kid in class dared me to do it. I knew my mother wouldn't buy it. So I kept silent. Questions about my homosexuality came up. They asked me if I liked boys. The counselor said it would be perfectly acceptable to say what I was feeling. The translator woman darted her eyes at the counselor when she hinted at any semblance of sympathy toward me. In the translator's eyes, I was the Devil, and gay children should not be allowed to think it was okay to get away with it scot-free. Every question about my homosexuality was deflected and denied with a terminating NO. Instead of facing the music, I chose to close up and decided at that moment I would hide my secret until I was free to move out at eighteen.

The one hour dragged on painfully slow, but in the end, my stoic determination won. The guidance counselor had other matters to attend to and dismissed us. I went home, and I didn't even cry. I locked it in and was determined to get through however many years of school I had left without getting into another situation of such colossal embarrassment.

Ten years later in that one therapy session, when I thought I was over it all, I felt like I was ten again. Hating the very nature of what made me *ME*. I couldn't believe my mother was still following me around even though I was not physically around her anymore.

The day yoga became an offering in school was a huge blessing that I wasn't aware of at the time. I had no idea what an anchor it would become for me.

I did my first ashtanga yoga class in acting school with Ezra Lebank, who was a junior while I was a freshman. In their year, they had daily yoga, and by the time our class moved up, they phased out the yoga program and introduced Alexander Technique, the Feldenkrais Method, modern dance and dynamic movement as part of our training. Little did I know I would go deep into the recesses of my psyche and completely redefine myself multiple times before graduation.

Ezra held weekly yoga classes for the underclassmen who were interested. It was such a brilliant complement to the other physical work we explored in our acting training. I felt a massive high from it. The rhythm was completely different to martial arts. My body ached all over the next day, but I felt so mentally focused. And it felt like I took a huge, emotion-clearing bath. I knew I needed more yoga in my life. I was hooked.

In the beginning, I was enamored with the physicality of yoga. The movements were strangely familiar and satiated my thirst for a challenge. Yet there was something about the flow of ashtanga that changed my emotions. The first year, I didn't quite understand what it was, nor did I care. I had so much going on at school with the looming threat of being kicked out from the acting program that I simply appreciated how yoga felt inside and out.

After sophomore year ended and I survived the second-year cut, I started to practice vinyasa yoga religiously. I went through a massive shift that allowed me to move through the last two years of school from a place of excitement rather than fear. Those three months of summer felt like a wild rollercoaster ride that would forever change me.

Unlike the summer before, I fled the country to escape having to spend time with my parents. After a year of massive internal deconstruction, I didn't want to be around anyone or anything familiar. Some of my classmates were auditioning for theatre festivals and doing anything that would help their resume. I instead applied to do a work exchange program abroad. It was either pay to volunteer and save the sea turtles in Costa Rica or make a wage as a bartender in a pub in England. I was too selfish at that point to pay to volunteer. The thought was ludicrous to me. So I spent my summer in England and Western Europe bartending and traveling in an attempt to escape my worries and fears.

The irony was that after two months, I was homesick, and would return two weeks earlier than expected. The backpacking life was not for me. Especially when I realized that no matter how much I traveled, I could not escape the issues of my own self-worth. I was studying to be an actor, but when I was in Edinburgh during the Fringe Festival, I didn't even care to go to the theatre. Something was way off. Backpacker or not, traveling with the intent to escape created an unavoidable feeling of being a fugitive on the run. Except what I was running from was not as thrilling as running from the law.

The summer that changed me forever started when my good friend from acting school, Diana, brought me and our mutual conservatory comrade in crime, Otis, to Jivamukti Yoga School in Union Square. Diana grew up in California and had a childhood full of meditation with her mother, and her mother was a master Reiki practitioner to boot. She was the first person like that I had ever met, and I was so fascinated with the way she experienced the world. She inspired me to connect more to life through the language of symbols and signs from the universe. It was a completely different way of being. During my high school years, I had aggressively resisted the Buddhist ways of my father and became an ardent supporter of atheism. I was quite surprised how quickly my belief systems were changing since the start of acting training. But I was also relieved that a more spiritually connected perspective made me feel more at ease and less on guard.

I don't remember whose idea it was, but all three of us were stoned when we went in to my first yoga class in a proper studio outside Purchase. I was still in my active state of rebelling against everything that my parents told me not to do. So, without much hesitation, we were all at the corner deli smoking conspicuously before class. A lot of my classmates were high during our somatic movement classes. I was too much of a prude to risk doing that before class, but school was out, so I made the quick decision to throw caution to the wind.

Otis has this unpredictably fun and larger-than-life personality. He has a way of infecting you with his cheerfulness, and we always found ourselves in very unexpected situations. A couple of months earlier, for spring break, we decided to go to Amsterdam together, just the two of us, since our friends thought it was too burdensome to make the seven-hour trip across the Atlantic. We smoked so much that we were often separated and spent most of our time drifting in crowds of random strangers who took us in. It was like they could smell the desperate self-loathing on my person and felt compelled to milk it further. The times when we did run into each other in the city center were when I was baked at the Van Gogh Museum and had to abruptly leave because I was overwhelmed by the pain popping out through the paint. A similar experience of unhealthy empathy took place when I lost my composure due to the tight confinement of the Anne Frank house. From one moment of debauchery to the next, I could not escape the pain evoked by the landmarks and history of the place.

However, on this big yoga day, I had a very cathartic experience that was quite different from the usual bouts of paranoia and sweeping sensations of indifference that smoking marijuana brought me. My first Jivamukti class was with Rima Rabbath, a slender Lebanese woman who spoke with an alluring raspy-ness that could capture anyone's attention. I don't remember the exact story she told that day, but I have fond memories of her opening class with inspiring childhood stories about growing up in war-torn Beirut. She oozed so much love and compassion that people flocked to her class by the dozens. There must have been fifty people in class that day; we were mat to mat. We started and ended class by chanting, *"Lokah samastah sukhino bhavantu,"* a Sanskrit chant that the Jivamukti founders, Sharon Gannon and David Life, translate as "May all beings everywhere be happy and free, and may the thoughts, words, and actions of my own life contribute in some way to that happiness and to that freedom for all."

As everyone piled out of the room and the class emptied out, the three of us stayed in our triangular mat formation, staring at the altar at the front of the classroom. "Wow," said Otis, as he widely grinned to break our silence. We all started to chuckle at the amazing beauty of our shared experience. Perhaps the incredible feeling was due to being in a communal space where everyone was moving and breathing with the intention of *lokah samastah sukhino bhavantu*. Maybe it was the weed, or the synchronicity of practicing together or both. I felt so connected to everyone in and outside the room. And, for the first time, I felt an unspeakable amount of love for myself and my friends who brought me to yoga.

I am neither advocating nor condemning the mind-altering capabilities of natural plants and plant medicine to change us. The *Yoga Sutras*, written around 400 CE, document the results of a disciplined spiritual yoga practice. Patanjali writes in the final chapter, "*Janmaushadhi mantra tapah samaadhi jaah siddhayah*," which translates as "Siddhis (psychic powers) are born of practices performed in previous births, or by herbs, mantra repetition, self-discipline or samadhi."[1]

It is the only mention in the *Yoga Sutras* about the use of plant medicine to attain an altered state of consciousness in the pursuit of psychic powers. In India, there is a sect of Sufi ascetics who use marijuana for clairvoyance. There are many artists and spiritual seekers, me being one of them, who have used plant medicines like marijuana recreationally or for inspirational purposes. Many Buddhist sages and yogic masters like Iyengar or Swami Prabhavananda have advised against the use of *aushadhi* ("plant medicine/herbs") to attain an altered state. These warnings are meant to keep abuse and dependency on external substances at bay, which is common sense.

Though I cannot help but note how blissful I felt practicing in an altered state of consciousness induced by cannabis, my realization

---

1   BKS Iyengar's translation of the Yoga Sutras in "Light on the Yoga Sutras of Patanjali," (Patanjala Yoga Pradipika), Thorsons, Hammersmith, 1966/1996, p 230.

was that intention and ceremony are very important in creating a spiritual experience, regardless of the use or non-use of substances. The moment in class that shifted our recreational use of cannabis to a spiritual experience was catalyzed through Rima's inspirational talk and the repetitive mantra chanting that completely shifted our inner mental and emotional spaces.

That would be my first foray into exploring the use of intoxicants to access a higher possibility. And that greater experience of peace and love was only accessible because of the kind of ceremony that the structure of the yoga class created. Through the chanting, and the constant reminder of moving and with the intention of each breath as an offering of peace, I quickly left the realm of being a recreational drug user to receive a higher spiritual experience that was previously unknown to me.

Since then, I sought to find that feeling again through practicing yoga without the use of substances. I never really liked the way my tongue would taste like a metal pipe when I smoked. I was more or less successful in experiencing a whole range of emotions without cannabis. I was hooked to the feeling at the end of class. At times, I found massive emotional releases; other times, I was able to abide in a consistent state of peace.

And I never felt the desire to smoke weed to recreate the connective high I felt that day with my friends. I wasn't looking to transcend my body or develop psychic powers; I just wanted to feel comfortable living my life as me. Something in me knew that the only real drug I needed was to be produced internally.

This was the catalytic moment that changed everything. I started to practice yoga two times a day for six days a week. Through meditation, I started to distinguish between the observer and the observed. I saw that I was not my pain, and that I was the creator of how attached I was to my comfort or displeasure. These were stories that I created in my head, and slowly, over time, I disengaged from them. That summer was a portal into a whole new world. I found myself going to crystal healings and *kirtan*, or chanting circles.

I even went to see Amma, the Indian hugging saint, who gives an energetic blessing in the form of a powerful hug while incanting a prayer in our ears. I swooned and fell to my knees in a complete daze. I returned to my seat, where another yoga teacher of mine, Narayani, who happened to be nearby, consoled me while I burst into a pool of tears. Through the simple hug of this compassionate and divinely empowered saint, my mind fell completely silent. I had no thoughts, and I felt a sublime emptiness that I had been yearning for.

I returned junior year of acting school to the shock of my classmates. Frantic, anxious Johnson was now a full-on yogi and a vegetarian to boot. I made drastic changes that summer because I was at a turning point of knowing that I couldn't go down the road of constant anxiety and depression. I did not want to fight so hard with myself anymore. I wanted to flow through the ups and downs of life with grace like all the beautiful teachers I had met. This was the beginning of realizing that flow and grace would be a daily choice I would have to make for a few years until feeling safe and at ease became natural again. I didn't care how drastic the changes were, or how some friends of mine were convinced I had joined a cult. Life changed, period. People who didn't support that eventually fell away from my life, and for the first time ever, I felt everything was really going to be okay.

CHAPTER 5

SELF-DISCOVERY: MINI AWAKENINGS THROUGH INTERNAL EXPLORATION

"Self-inquiry is not asking you to believe or to trust—it is putting a mirror in front of you and asking you to look."

MOOJJI

In conjunction with weekly yoga, we studied the Alexander Technique and the Feldenkrais Method—two systems designed by two different men who took the road less traveled when it came to conventionality. Over my four years at Purchase College, it was from these classes of self-inquiry with my somatic movement teachers that I discovered how inextricably linked my psychological and emotional triggers were interwoven into my physical body.

Frederick Alexander was this Shakespearean actor in the late 1800s who repeatedly lost his voice during unamplified performances. After seeking medical advice to no avail, he concluded that he was unintentionally hurting his voice while speaking. Through experimentation and self-observation, he realized his issues were rooted in an unconscious patterning of physical posture, poor breathing and inefficient use of his supportive musculature.

Moshé Feldenkrais came a few decades later. He was an Israeli engineer in the early 1900s who created a method to increase self-awareness through movement. His refusal to accept his old soccer knee injury was the impetus for his developing a way to self-rehabilitate. His whole theory was that "thought, feeling, perception and movement are closely interrelated and influence each other."

My Alexander Technique teacher, Gwen Ellis, and Feldenkrais teacher, Forrestine Paulay, were pivotal in expanding my field of consciousness. They guided my first introductions to deepening my awareness through somatic inquiry. The study of somatics highlights the internal experience of physical movement, deriving from the Greek word *somatikos* (or "body"). It's essentially exploring the sensations and perceiving them from within, which can only happen through developing deeper states of concentration and expanded mindfulness.

Later on, in my studies as a yoga teacher, these concepts came full circle for me as I couldn't help but notice the parallels between the type of work I studied during acting training and the ancient tools of wisdom that yogis taught for centuries. After all, theatre has its roots in religious ritual. As the forefathers of theatre created stories and represented them onstage to pay homage to the gods, there is no doubt in my mind that these actors became channels of the sacred. And in order to get there, knowingly or unknowingly they had to draw their senses inward to discover their authentic individual expressions of divinity. Drawing the senses inward through somatic inquiry is very much analogous to the fifth limb of the eight limbs of yoga, *pratyahara*. Pratyahara is the practice of controlling all the senses as a precursor to achieving states of meditation and moving into states of spiritual consciousness.

I was always excited to head to Alexander Technique with Gwen. She was the embodiment of sweetness. From the way she carried herself to the way she spoke. She floated into the classroom with an ease that was inspiring. She walked as if she didn't carry an ounce of stress on her. Even her skin looked different. It had the glow of being light and unburdened. Every time she opened her mouth, it was like the heavens parted and an angel graced us with compassionate kindness. There was something about the Alexander Technique and Gwen that gave me permission to unhook myself from my heavy baggage. The verbal cuing in her class was really my first foray into self-development and evolution. My first-year acting teacher, Dale Moffitt, made it explicitly clear that acting was not about therapy. But I always felt so light and free after Gwen's class. How could the therapeutic aspects of the theatre not be considered?

Our first day as freshmen in her class, she had us lie down on our backs with a thin, novel-sized book as a support pillow. With simple and precise cuing, she guided us to find our optimal length in the neck while softening the jaw. She carefully chose words that didn't feel like instruction. It felt like she went inside the words to create a visceral conversation with my neck. "Hey, do you want to grip and hold on with that much tension? Is it really necessary?" The cuing was more sophisticated and more structured than my colloquial portrayal here, though her verbal cues always felt relatable. Like she and my neck were two close friends giving each other advice, and shortly after, there was a remarkable surrender and release. And like when a close friend tells the truth straight without any pretense, I was often caught off guard by how exposed I felt. Through each surprise shedding of tears on the cold, gray floor in Alexander class, I entered the first stages of learning how to surrender by acknowledging my emotional baggage.

Acknowledgment for each person is a unique and essential step on the spiritual journey. If I had come out of class in denial that I was in any way responsible for creating my own tensions, or if I understood that I was the creator of my physical tensions and chose to relapse into the same stress patterns, then I would be in a very different place in life right now. Acknowledgment is the forerunner of change. Inversely, denial is the stubborn resistance to any kind of shift. Even worse, it reinforces our internal programs of monotony.

At the time, I wasn't sure if it was the manual release of the neck and shoulders or all the yawning exercises that relaxed my jaw. My Linklater voice teacher, Craig Bacon, gave us full permission to yawn whenever we wanted. He said it helped to release jaw and tongue tension while promoting deeper diaphragmatic breathing. Yawning bigger meant bigger releases. It was the first time I had been told by any academic authority that yawning was acceptable. In voice class, yawning was equivalent to letting go.

Training to be an actor might sound like going to massage school—as if we were studying to express the fullness of our physicality through embodied anatomy training. Except we were also learning how to unravel conditioned imprints that stemmed from years of psychological habits.

I had sense enough not to tell my parents I was paying thousands of dollars to learn how to yawn without inhibition during my first week. My mom had the strange impression that my daily class routine would involve Hollywood stunt training. Even though I had assured her I was safe in acting school, every phone conversation was a constant reminder that I wasn't in a Peking Opera–style martial arts training program. "I'm not training to be Jackie Chan, Mom." "Then what are you learning, then?" Those were always interesting conversations.

I dreaded acting scene study, Lecoq, clown and speech class. These classes were performance based, and I feared falling flat on my face in front of my classmates. This was a fear I had not learned to let go of yet. The fear that I irredeemably sucked, that I wasn't good enough, and that I didn't deserve to be there was overwhelming. It seemed that all of my classmates, and almost everyone in my conservatory, went to competitive performing-arts high schools and they were onstage from the moment they could utter, "Scene." The first week of freshman year, everyone talked about all the top conservatories they auditioned for, like Julliard, NYU Tisch, Carnegie Mellon, Boston Conservatory, and the list goes on. I remember the freshman inquisition clearly. There were many conversations where my classmates and the upperclassmen would size everyone up by learning which schools we were accepted into, and, by default, they could figure out which ones we were rejected from.

The truth was, I went to SUNY Geneseo the year before, in the middle of nowhere, Upstate New York, because I was trying to get away from my parents and actually had no clue as to a major. During my time there, I decided to audition for SUNY Purchase without any education on how competitive getting into an acting conservatory would be. I was actually waitlisted and surprisingly received my letter of acceptance two months after everyone else got theirs. I had not applied to other schools like my cohorts. I was selected from a pool of semi-desirable leftovers. Or maybe I was part of some diversification ploy for more Asian blood. I entered my four years of training with my glass half full, always operating with the mentality that I was the school's sloppy seconds.

My theatre vocabulary was extremely elementary compared to my classmates. I wasn't up to date with what was happening on Broadway and was still a virgin to classic American playwrights. The theatre I did was the amateur non-performing-arts-high-school kind of theatre where the after-school budget was spent on the science and math clubs instead. I went to the extremely cerebral and specialized Townsend Harris High School in Flushing, Queens, and my parents counted on my becoming a doctor, lawyer or private banker. Townsend Harris was definitely not known for its theatre program.

So, when I had this peculiar divine intervention prompting me to audition for the acting conservatory, it was a curveball. I remember that odd day vividly, as anyone would if time seemingly stopped and the sky split open with a specific message for them. I was hanging out with my friend, Brady, at Geneseo. She was the exuberant, musical-theatre type who flitted around campus in her long, tie-dye frocks, happily singing show tunes. We were in her dorm room lounging. She was humming away, doing something on her laptop, and I was staring out into the hills where the sun met the Genesee Valley, a.k.a. where boredom met nothingness. Then, all of a sudden, my eyes were drawn to the window. I picked myself out of the bed, and all my attention was brought to this massive opening in the clouds. Sunlight rained through the crack in the sky. It was like that moment in *The Lion King* when Simba was born and the entire animal kingdom gathered to watch the universe shine its glorious light over his head. Then a massive download of information entered me. I can only describe it as a booming voice that didn't speak in words. I thought I had gone insane for a moment. I didn't hear it with my physical ears; I received a message through feelings and images.

The experience was entirely weird and supernatural. In those few seconds when the universe pulled my attention away from the doldrums, I saw the blueprint of my next four years. It was as if the universe was tired of watching me wallow in indecisiveness and decided to push me onto a different path.

I turned to Brady, who knew everything about theatre, and seemingly out of the blue asked her which acting schools I should apply to. She was pleasantly surprised, as she didn't think I took theatre seriously and it seemed rather abrupt coming from me. But she enthusiastically took on the role of audition coach and started to name all the top private conservatories. All of which had massive tuitions. She then told me about SUNY Purchase. There are over sixty SUNY (State University of New York) campuses across New York State, and I had never even heard of SUNY Purchase. She likened it to the poor man's Julliard. "They have a very good theatre program, and I can help you pick your monologues and songs. How exciting!" So, in that moment, without any confusion, I decided to audition for a professional actor training program.

I had a mini freak-out knowing that I had to do a song and a classical monologue; Shakespeare terrified me at the time. I ended up doing a contemporary monologue from *The Laramie Project* and one from *The Misanthrope*. Fortunately, it was acceptable to do Molière's French satire in lieu of Shakespeare. It was a lot more digestible to me at the time. I can't even remember my song choice. I blocked it out. Whatever it was, it must have been some patter song that Brady wisely picked out to hide the fact that I was by no means a singer.

At SUNY Geneseo, I explored a hodgepodge of majors. I was studying Spanish and going for a minor in piano pedagogy with the dream of traveling the world and studying abroad. It was the perfect agenda devised by my aspiring inner escape artist. I would run away to the south of Spain or Paris and absorb the sophistication and elegance of European culture. I had a European romance storyline scripted out and was just itching to play out the fantasy. But it seemed that destiny had other plans for me.

Instead, I voluntarily signed up for the Hogwarts School of Deconstructing My Soul. That's what it felt like to me, anyway. I had such a superficial understanding of what acting was. I thought it was about putting on a mask, playing pretend and assuming a persona that was not my own. It was a way for me to hide and escape from all my issues. At the start, acting meant seeking refuge from who I truly was.

It was a rude awakening when all of the classes and my teachers challenged the very way I was conditioned to make choices in my life. Everything we were taught in our classes was delivered with the purpose of helping us find carte blanche, so that we could build a character from a place of neutrality. Theoretically, I understood that our own habits and patterns could be problematic if it didn't suit the character, but it was a much more difficult journey than I had imagined.

Naturally, I developed a partiality to my movement classes. I didn't have to talk or be graded for my zoo of a Brooklyn-Queens-Chinese-New York speech pattern. My movement classes were coveted sacred time where I was given permission to explore my mind-body connection. I was able to express myself through the skin and bones and through the unoppressive medium of movement. All of the cathartic mental, psychological and emotional realizations from that were incredible bonuses.

I have a fond memory of hanging out with my other classmates in our dorm making energy balls. And no, we weren't rolling up cacao powder and dates into nutritious, bite-sized snacks. We were literally playing with energy through our hands, practicing what Forrestine Paulay, our Feldenkrais teacher, had taught us.

We were a weird bunch. After stage combat class, we would run around campus improvising Jerry Springer–inspired "my baby daddy" domestic violence scenes, screaming and cursing at each other while throwing fake slaps, punches and kicks. To the point where it was so convincing that some poor believer would call campus police out of concern. "We're studying for our stage combat exam. We're in the acting program." The campus police never looked very amused.

Post-stage-combat silliness, we retreated to our dorm to have an energy ball party where we used our hands like scanners along the contours of each other's bodies. A group of about eight of us moved together in a symbiotic dance of entangled bodies, slowly sensing our way around each other's electromagnetic fields. "Whoa, can you feel that?" "I definitely feel a lot of energy coming from the back of your hips." "Can you feel my energy ball?" "I definitely feel something, but I think it's a different kind of ball." Our deep moments of introspection and self-examination were always chock-full of witty one-liners and smart-aleck banter. Never a dull moment with that bunch.

We always kept ourselves entertained and got jealous looks from the liberal arts students who didn't make it into the conservatory program. "Oh, there are those pompous acting conservatory assholes seeking attention again." You could feel them thinking that. It pretty much kept an incestuous dynamic between those of us in the conservatory.

Forrestine Paulay's Feldenkrais class was a three-hour awareness-through-movement class once a week after dinner. My freshman class of twenty-two aspiring actors was definitely split into three factions when it came to Forrestine. There were the interested, the indifferent, and the disinterested who fell asleep during most of the movement explorations. I never understood why they never clicked with her. If Gwen was an angelic healer from heaven, then Forrestine was a shamanic sorceress from the mysterious forest. She not only taught Feldenkrais but was also a modern dancer back in her heyday and had a PhD in Gestalt work, while being a practitioner of Laban movement analysis, kinesiology, cranio-sacral therapy, psychotherapy and osteopathy. At that point in time, to me she was an all-around magical conundrum who I looked up to with veneration and awe.

In her seventies, she had a wonderful bush of silver hair and reminded me of Bea Arthur, except when she opened her mouth and spoke with this silky, mystical voice. She was nimble for her age and would shock the class when she plowed her legs over her head and effortlessly went into the splits. But it wasn't the impressiveness of her flexibility that got me hooked on what she was teaching. It was everything underneath the surface that could be felt and not seen.

The day Forrestine started dowsing our auras with a pendulum was the day she lost half of the class. People made fun of her for being a witch, but I was mesmerized. Dowsing is a divination tool that traditionally uses a gemstone pendulum to locate water, gold or other minerals. It was a tool used in early medical diagnoses. However, she used her pendulum to show us where we were energy deficient in the context of stage presence for the actor. But I knew there was something deeper going on. She was trying to help us heal. I realize now that only when you dive right into your baggage without avoiding it can presence be fully expressed. Presence doesn't come from avoidance and an escapist approach to life.

She worked with one of our classmates from Oklahoma, who busted his shoulder in an accident. She laid him down in front of the class and used him as an example of how trauma could affect someone's electromagnetic field, or aura. She then started to do energy work on him. I watched him convulse and twitch in reaction to her osteopathic bodywork on his shoulder and arm. No one knew what to make of it. Was she doing an exorcism or something? Was this real? Were his convulsions just to mess with us? It was the first time we had seen anything like that. Little did I know I would be doing bodywork on clients four short years later when I met my mentor, Courtney Bauer, creator of Curriculum AUM and founder of Studio ANYA. She would help me to metamorphose into a professional twitcher.

Twitching, shaking, tremoring, from how I understand it through my own body and witnessing my clients over the years, is simply a release mechanism. I like to think of the human body as a tree. Just as the rings of a tree record the lush seasons of rain and the dry spells, our connective tissue, muscles, and bones remember everything just as vividly. Even though we may think we are over something because we worked it out in the mind with reason and logic, we forget to let the body and heart digest what has happened. Forrestine simply brought his consciousness to the point of injury, and to his and everyone's surprise, his body expressed how it felt about the past trauma. It was as if his body was twitching a short story in Morse code. Like it was telling us how upset and disturbed it was from the accident. I secretly wanted to be worked on next, but the fear of what might come out to my classmates kept my enthusiasm at bay.

I really wanted to put a cap on my emotions, or everyone would think I was this volatile and aloof person. My terrible poker face didn't really help. In high school, I was the loner with a small group of friends. No one really bothered me as I had erected a massive emotional fortress around me and went through my day-to-day repressed and in constant fear of being found out. In college, I became an unpredictable boiling pot of emotions. Sometimes in movement explorations, I would break into nonstop maniacal laughter or, as others told me, giggles on crack. Other times, I fumed in anger, trying to keep it hidden in the shadows. Or I would ugly-cry with snot dripping into my teeth. I wasn't able to apply any of this raw emotion to my acting work in an authentic way yet, and it was very hard for me to reconcile that.

Forrestine not only had a flair for what we perceived as sorcery in our naiveté, she was also anatomically precise and specific with her use of language in expressing it. Sadly, she was only on campus two short years. Maybe word got out to the administration that we were hoodooing and voodooing our way through movement class with no apparent application to the craft of acting. Direct application or not, it was enormously helpful on my path towards self-realization.

Before our precise anatomical explorations, she used diagrams of the skeleton to teach us the connection of the pelvis, spine and cranium. Anatomy in biology class during high school was purely memorization from an intellectual standpoint. Here, she was teaching us how to live anatomy, not study it. She put us in a fetal position on the floor where we undulated our spines from our tailbones all the way to our skulls. The few people who were mostly stoned during class would writhe around making weird noises. Others straight up passed out from dinner-food comas and sheer exhaustion from the volume of work required of us. I, on the other hand, felt like a snake writhing in my skin, trying to break free from the chains that bogged me down. Every time I tried to create more precision in the rippling of the spinal movement, I felt heat rising from my tailbone to my head.

A few years later I recognized this as the beginning of the kundalini rising. Kundalini is a yogic term referring to the latent reservoir of energy potential in each person, which manifests as energy rising through the physical body. Think of it as the creative spark that caused the Big Bang. It's essentially *THE* creative force. It's the thunderbolt shooting out of the sky. It's the energy that makes babies. It's the inspiration that powers artists to express. Everyone has it, but it only operates at a fraction of our energetic potential. In yogic texts, when kundalini is fully activated, superhuman abilities start to manifest, such as telepathy, clairvoyance, healing, precognition and other psychic abilities. Kundalini activates from the perineum, at the pelvic floor, and ascends through the sacrum, then the spinal column, eventually illuminating the entire brain.

In my case, the repetitive spinal undulations in a fetal position targeting the tailbone was an important key in developing the awareness to unlock my kundalini. The vibrations of energy that rose through the stiff points of my spine could express fury or great sadness. This was a process of consciously witnessing and transmuting old stories. But I didn't know this at the time. I was aroused and then ashamed that I could be aroused when doing a Feldenkrais exercise. With all the movement happening in my pelvis, it was inevitable that I would experience sexual energy. I know now that it is perfectly natural and that my shame about it was a layer of conditioning that needed to be addressed.

These movement exercises in my somatic explorations were designed to be a conscious reclaiming of my creative and sexual energy, which really is one and the same. They highlighted my repressed sexuality. They highlighted my feelings of rejection and emotional abandonment by my parents. What boggled my mind was that these stories were stored physically as lower-back tension and tightness in the hips.

Acknowledging the root of these physical sensations created a profound internal dialogue long after graduation. *How did this happen? When did it happen? I thought I dealt with these issues, so why is it still causing me discomfort? Have I really completely let go of these issues?*

Somatic movement training in acting school was designed to make us discover ourselves by asking deeper and more meaningful questions so that we could become better actors. In the process, it inadvertently taught me how to connect more deeply with my emotional and physical pain and how to release it. And release only happened when I asked difficult questions and, moreover, lived the questions without obsessing over the answers. This part of the journey was not always easy, nor particularly graceful, but it gave me the foundation of self-inquiry that became the framework through which I would experience this new world of spirituality that I unknowingly entered.

CHAPTER 6

ARCHETYPAL PATTERNS: THE HUMAN STORY

"The archetype is a figure—be it a daemon, a human being, or a process—that constantly recurs in the course of history and appears wherever creative fantasy is freely expressed. Essentially, therefore, it is a mythological figure . . . In each of these images there is a little piece of human psychology and human fate, a remnant of the joys and sorrows that have been repeated countless times in our ancestral history."

CARL JUNG

With all of my soul-searching, I was still confused at how to reconcile all the different aspects of myself that were speaking out of turn. A voice teacher once told me that the average person changes the pitch of how they speak seventy-seven times per day depending on the environment and what they want from those around them. Typically, when we shift our vocal pitch down an octave, it shows dominance, while higher pitches reflect everything from submissiveness to excitement. That is a lot of characters to juggle. The part that was most difficult for me to embrace was not so much the vast panel of archetypes living within me as it was the darker parts of myself. How could I accept them as useful parts of my whole self if I was choosing to live a spiritual path?

On my nineteenth birthday in New Orleans, I lost my virginity in the back of a jeep during a reckless explosion of unexpected excitement with a complete stranger. The fantasy of being swept away in a cloud of romance was replaced instead by an inebriated carnal lust. I never thought that was how it would go down. I had forever changed. And I returned from spring break with an unapologetic disposition to say yes to things that I once categorized as unacceptable. This began my examination of my value system and how I could cope with my dark side.

Like many gay men, I found myself in a series of casual sexual relationships. Secretly, my inner idealist held out for the fabricated Hollywood fairy tale we were taught to love. Yet there was always a voice telling me that I was undeserving of happiness and that it was not for my kind. The raw, unfiltered part of me was determined to have it and impatiently strived to make it happen. I decided to fight for it. And I didn't want to wait. Since I was a teenager, I felt I was missing out on life, and I was envious of those who were in young, straight relationships. I deserved to be with someone too, even if it meant we were a complete mismatch.

In my late-bloomed angst and emotion, I started my quest for "the one." However, my idea of who I should be attracted to was corrupted by how media portrayed masculinity. I had this impression that I was the softer and feminine gay, without having any grasp on the depths of a gay relationship. I wrote off any guy who demonstrated effeminate behavior. In the beginning, I would only involve myself with guys who slipped under the gaydar. The paranoid part of me always switched on when I was on a date in public, fearing that I'd be found out.

My inexperienced younger self was a perfectionist. And, in grasping for the perfect ideal, I became superficial and attracted the wrong type of men. Men who were carrying equally damaged psychologies. Like the law of attraction, and in accord with what the ancient yogis say about the external world reflecting our internal world, I constantly encountered the counterpart to my issues. Each time my heart was broken, I saw the universe being unfair and playing games with me. Now, I see those times as missed opportunities that could have potentially resolved some issues, instead of painfully duplicating in my relationships the stories of seeking validation from my abusive childhood.

It is in this spirit of Thomas Merton, where "no man is an island," that we must seek to understand the human story as our own story. We must seek to understand that our struggles and hardships are shared by all. This is the only way to heal and to evolve out of our loneliness and despair. One of the ways I looked back on my childish acts of young love was through the eyes of the Jungian archetypes.

I first was made aware of the four main archetypes—the child, victim, prostitute and saboteur—junior year in movement class. It wasn't until I studied the *atmatypes* (a hybrid of the Sanskrit "soul" [*atma*] and the Jungian concept of *archetype*) through the AUM curriculum created by my mentor, Courtney Bauer, a couple of years later, that I fully understood how important the archetypal work was to my spiritual development. Without getting into the intricacies of psychology, the key takeaway from delving into the realm of archetypes is the inevitable sense of belonging to the human story.

When we acknowledge ourselves in others and others in ourselves, a bridge of compassion is formed. We are no longer alone. I see no way forward other than accepting this simple yet difficult lesson of embodying compassion for ourselves and our fellow humans through story. Despite the details of our journeys being unique, every person can relate to the universality of the archetypal lessons.

Unlike stereotypes, which are oversimplified preconceived notions, archetypes are universal patterns that are repeated in human behavior. The prostitute is a Jungian archetype that has existed since the beginning of recorded civilization. I would argue that it is the most vilified of all the archetypes. I often wonder if people are disgusted by the idea of whores doing business because it reflects an aspect of themselves they detest. Does the prostitute's willing surrender of self-respect remind us of times when we were put in a situation where we sold ourselves out?

The expressions of being a "sell-out" or "whoring yourself out" in our culture highlight the shadow aspect of the prostitute where integrity is compromised. When we are put in situations where we are forced to concede the guiding principles that govern our lives, we become the shadow aspect of the prostitute.

The concessions do not necessarily have to be sexual in nature. It could be a concession of our ideas or talents in exchange for something else like power or money. We see this in many people who give up their dreams for a financially stable career. If we all learn to accept this archetypal pattern and empathize with how every person in this world has had to trade away something they stand for, then perhaps we would not be as judgmental toward ourselves and each other.

During my naïve search for my other half, I often felt depressingly incomplete. One could say I was in love with love itself. Sometimes, for the sake of just being with someone, I allowed the fear of being alone to rule my actions. When it clearly wasn't a match, I would throw myself desperately at my lover and make myself overly available. In other relationships, the exact opposite would happen as a gesture of revenge. I would close up after a few weeks of intimacy and erase them from my life completely. It was this bizarre battle of negotiating how I valued myself.

This "Love me, love me not" attitude eventually tired itself out. Everyone has a breaking point. Having my heart broken five times or more by that point, I started the very necessary process of understanding my craving for instant gratification and my secret desire for self-imprisonment. It all boiled down to an investigation into my self-doubt and fears. Here, my inner prostitute became an ally. I rechanneled the carefree and seductive qualities of the prostitute to listen to my heart and not my mind. The types of people I attracted into my life changed. They were not quite the right match, but at least they were not using me physically, emotionally and energetically.

This period of constantly seeking approval undeniably also involved my wounded child, victim and saboteur. It created emotional ambiguity and messiness. The wounded little boy in me heightened this messiness by still carrying around the pain of my family story. My victim constantly lingered in the comfortable world of feeling abused and being kept small. Unconsciously, I was addicted to pity. The saboteur hounded me time and time again with how undeserving and unworthy I was. "I'm not a good actor." "I will never be an obedient son," so "I'm not deserving of love." I was aware of these voices on a daily basis, but unsure of how to quiet them.

It wasn't until I experienced past-life regressions through dreams and shamanic journeying that I realized my behavioral patterns spanned lifetimes of playing variations of the prostitute. I played this role countless times as the coy vixen, the seductress, the temptress or the dark enchantress. Through visions from meditations, journeys or dreams, I witnessed my old selves repeatedly concocting love potions to conquer an unrequited love. It came from a place of wanting to control. In one vivid past-life memory, I was a Mongolian princess who overtly disobeyed her father's orders, eloped, was caught, and then put to death for disobedience. This archetypal pattern replayed itself in my current life through rebellion from the traditional family unit, fear of rejection, and the unwavering desire to be loved.

Whether the memories are historically accurate or not and who I was exactly at that point in history is beside the point. It's the images and the significance of the lessons taught through these symbols that matter. At one point, I was obsessed with figuring out the exact details, which led to me getting lost in the details of a past long gone instead of using these memories to live my life fully in the present moment. Past-life memories can be as real as you allow them to be. And I find them most useful when we can learn from them like fables that are transmitting lessons.

More recently, in 2015, I received a Nadi-leaf reading from a Tamil astrologer, Mr. Kumar. After presenting my thumbprint to the astrologer, he checked his archives to find a bundle of leaves that matched my thumbprint before asking me a series of yes-or-no questions that needed to be verified before he could read my leaf.

Without any information, the astrologer told me my parents' names, and my father's birth name, which had been legally changed many years ago. To my surprise, he also recounted specific facts that I had to verify as true. He knew the name of my current partner, what I majored in college, how many siblings I had, my relationship with them, the kind of career I had, and the crossroads I was at in trying to move countries to start over. My inner skeptic wondered if he had hired a private investigator to collect facts on me. As he verified more and more details about my current life, I let that theory go, and openly listened to his forecast of my future. He touched on milestones in my late thirties, forties and fifties that seemed very grand. Everything about my leaf was about my service to humanity's spiritual evolution.

Each line would be chanted in ancient Tamil, followed by an English translation. The one thing that caught me off guard—and it seemed it caught him off guard as well—was when he said that the only reason I am in same-sex relationships is because of past-life karma. And in the most mystical of ways, like something out of *The Lord of the Rings*, he ended the reading by telling me that if the time came for me to want more information, another leaf would be made available for me.

The accuracy of my present-life reading prompted me to delve deeper into my past-life leaf reading a few years later during January 2019. In Nadi astrology, it is believed that the past, present and future lives of all humans were recorded on palm leaves. Nadi astrologers were entrusted with the art and responsibility of reading these leaves as the sacred duty was passed down from generation to generation.

This was the first past-life reading from an external source I ever had. In the past, I was never able to attain a successful reading from any practitioners I came across. In fact, many doors were closed to me despite my incessant knocking. But I was no longer in a mental space where I was obsessing over the details. I took the story Mr. Kumar told me as simply that—a story with different layers of lessons.

He reported that the most immediate past life carrying the most karma in my current life was directly related to the lifetime I lived as a wealthy man born to the warrior caste in some forgotten Tamil kingdom a couple hundred years ago. I mistreated my servants by abusing them and underpaying them. I stole land from the temples. And I made a bad habit of being a promiscuous womanizer who broke hearts. According to the leaf, one of the girls who I promised to marry from a lower caste committed suicide because I reneged on my word. Before she killed herself, she cursed me so that I would never hurt another woman in the way she had been hurt again. This was the karmic explanation for me being reborn gay in this lifetime. This for sure made me ponder the ongoing debate as to whether homosexuality is a choice. In this case, according to Hindu reincarnation, I was cursed and needed to atone.

To release myself of this karmic imprint, a series of pilgrimages to various temples in Tamil was prescribed to me. I could not help but remember another psychic years ago telling me that in my mid-thirties there would be a massive energetic shift where I could choose to be with women if I wanted to. So the thought passed through my mind: *Will I still be gay if I do an energetic clearing of my so-called curse? Do I even want to go through with it? Am I so attached to my sexuality that I cannot see beyond the true meaning of the 'curse'?*

Past-life karma is like the debt collector knocking on your door, demanding you pay the interest accrued. After careful deliberation, I realized that atoning for the curse was really about making amends to all the pain and suffering that I caused in a lifetime where I abused control and was seduced by power. Mr. Kumar said that the issues I currently faced in my relationship would be alleviated once I released the past once and for all. I *do* have issues of over-asserting control and power, especially in relationships with my family and my partner. When I make my rounds on my temple pilgrimage later this year, it will be with the intention to clear the imprints of being overly controlling in all aspects of my current life. The purpose and only point of discovering our past-life stories is to apply the lessons to our current lives. Our individual consciousnesses are like colorful threads weaving a cosmic tapestry. Each of these threads are like memories long gone and can only be interpreted like remembering a dream. We can extract the essence of these remembrances to uncover unconscious motifs that keep us in a perpetual loop.

In yogic philosophy, this is known as *samskara*—our literal or figurative scars and battle wounds from previous lifetimes that inform our behaviors in this lifetime. These patterns will continue to manifest until we become conscious of the source and break free from the cycle. Like our DNA, which we inherit from our mother and father, we also inherit *samskara*. These mental and emotional blueprints directly impact the way we deal with life. In other words, our conditioned programming impedes our evolution of consciousness.

Consciousness is a palpable experience that is shared among the collective family. It moves and breathes as we all move and breathe. Every time we change the way we think or the way we live in our bodies, no matter how big or small the change, we cause ripples in the unified web and affect the whole forever.

This can be seen very clearly through the collective pain and suffering of any minority people. Ostracized communities can be reflected in my parents' rejection of me being me. The archetypal pattern of the parental unit rejecting the child comes to life, and energetic imprints of these *samskaras* are passed down to every single member of the affected party.

I can never pretend to understand what it feels like to inherit the generations of pain and suffering that are deeply felt in the ostracized communities of African Americans or the marginalized indigenous peoples of the Americas and Australia. However, my deep understanding of my personal obstacles and triumphs gives me a compassionate awareness of the archetypal patterns that I share with every single person who has ever experienced suffering.

The choices we make as people or as society at large can be encapsulated by our intrinsic desire to feel like we belong—to feel that we are cared for and loved. It all goes downhill when we allow the ancient survival program of our reptilian brain to fill us with fear. Fear of death or the unknown is the basis of all our fears. The fight-or-flight response is very useful when we are being chased by a bear, but when we transfer that mode of compulsive reaction into making life choices about our relationships, money, love and career, it proves troublesome.

This is why the art of mindful storytelling through theatre, film and various other artistic mediums is so important in bringing us closer to our mutual understanding of each other. When I see myself mirrored on stage through a touching piece of theater or when I resonate with the themes of elevated literature, I immediately feel less alone, and more connected to humanity. I have realized that every story of human triumph is unique but, at the same time, not. Nevertheless, our stories are really all the same if we consider that the underlying roadblocks are always rooted in the four basic archetypes of survival.

When we have made this realization, what then? How does acknowledging the sameness of all our stories allow us to move into our fullest potentials?

I like to think of it like gambling. I have never had a gambling problem; however, I know what it is like to be addicted to a craving. We have to figure out how much longer we want to play the game.

How long before we decide to step away from the metaphorical slot machine or the blackjack table? It's a matter of making a defining life choice, and taking brave action to free ourselves from the tapestry of lies and deceit that we've been entangled in. Then all the investigating and psychoanalysis and dependency fades away because we're living freely in the moment, right here, right now.

CHAPTER 7

THE POLARITIES OF SELF AND EMBRACING MY INNER REBEL

ॐ

"The Rebel does not believe in anything except his own experience. His truth is his only truth; no prophet, no messiah, no savior, no holy scripture, no ancient tradition can give him his truth."

OSHO

For as long as I can remember, I felt an undeniable urge to go against the grain. I always challenged others—not to be difficult but because it was in my nature to inquire and investigate the truth. There were times when my inner rebel was out of control, but once I learned to befriend him, I was able to deepen my experiences because the voices of self-judgment and self-criticism were silenced.

During my days of experimentation, I have a vivid memory of being high on substances that shall go unnamed with a few friends from school. We were in the East Village and brought forth the wrath of a bouncer at a club who was not impressed. I playfully went into the women's bathroom, chasing down my friends to get another hit, when a towering black man forcibly dragged me out of the bar. I was floating on bubbles. And when you're tripping, bubbles feel very real. It was nearly impossible to drag me up the stairs. He struggled as I burst out into body rolls like I was doing an interpretative dance of water personified. Then I transformed into the gay Rosa Parks. Instead of refusing to sit at the back of the bus, I challenged the political correctness of going into gender-specific bathrooms. I challenged the oppression of his blackness against the oppression of being me, a gaysian American. "I'm a minority of the minority. I'm the cream of the crop when it comes to minority status," I proclaimed. "Stop taking your issues of control and power out on me!" The only thing stopping his fist knocking me out was the other bouncer and my friends forming a circle of protection around my loose lips. The poor guy was just following the rules and doing his job of keeping things in order. But something in me delighted in pushing his buttons.

In astrology, my Uranus is in Sagittarius. Uranus is the planet in charge of radical shifts and rebellion. This alignment generates a vehement opposition in me toward obsolete and antiquated modes of being. All throughout my childhood into high school, I constantly triggered my parents and pushed other people's buttons, including some teachers who were baffled by my deferential way of undermining their authority. I loved playing the opponent for kicks—maybe because I knew my teachers weren't allowed to physically beat me. I developed a passion for eyebrow-raising questions in class, especially English literature and American history. I loved carrying the torch when it came to issues of justice or integrity, especially when it supported the underdog.

While most of my peers got quick thrills in garish and obvious ways, you would never know by looking at me how seditious I could really be. If I didn't agree with something, I made it known in some way or another. Most of the time, it could never be traced back to me, and I relished in the thrill of that.

Not only did I try my parents' patience on countless occasions, but also, on Sunday mornings, I could be found consistently cheating on my Chinese school recitation exams. It was my way of saying "screw you" to my parents for sending me to school on a Sunday. Every week, there would be a recitation test where we had to regurgitate cryptic Chinese poetry on paper. It felt senseless and impractical to learn the equivalent of what Old English is to modern-day English.

I really despised it. *How is it going to be useful for me to learn how to read hieroglyphics?* I thought learning to read and write Chinese was an unnecessarily difficult and futile task. I only spoke Chinese at home and at Sunday school with the other Cantonese-speaking ABCs (American-born Chinese) kids, while my siblings and I conversed in English in regular school. My father kept telling me that in twenty years Chinese would be the main language used in business around the world, and that I would rue the day I didn't obey him. I secretly vowed that I would never be a Chinese-speaking business man.

There were countless moments when I talked back to Mom or Dad about the uselessness of what they were making me do.

"The other kids don't have to go to school on Sunday. You chose to move to America. Why do I have to be forced to learn Chinese?" I demanded.

"Your face is Chinese. Your blood is Chinese. You will learn Chinese. End of story!"

Even knowing that there was rarely any kind of negotiation about these things and that the conversation would be followed by an inevitable beating, I could never contain my outright objection to their impositions on me.

But I wasn't always comfortable that it was in my nature to incessantly question and doubt everything ever told me. Throughout my teenage years and into my early twenties, an internal voice criticized that part of me as "bad." It would be a while before I could unapologetically own my opinionated personality. And it was my exploration of how to more gracefully express my dissatisfaction with what was "right" or mainstream that brought me closer to real self-acceptance. Learning how to filter and finesse every impulse to play the contrarian was an entirely different lesson.

At seven, Mom and Dad decided to move us from Midwood, Brooklyn, without so much a conversation with us. One day we were in Brooklyn, and all of a sudden, we were living in a new apartment that we had not even visited before. There was no consideration for how me and my siblings felt about the matter. What about our friends? What about us just getting the hang of life as we were accustomed to it up to that point? Their lack of transparency was another example of how they played out the horrors they suffered as casualties of Communist China. We were their property, and our opinions were insignificant.

Mom and Dad closed down their successful fish market in Brooklyn, and we moved to Jamaica Avenue under the J train. Life was a bit calmer and less eventful living above our Chinese grocery store, which sold more shelf items and less live fish. My parents had saved up enough money to purchase a three-story building with two apartments and a shop space on the ground floor. We rented out one of the apartments and lived on the third floor. My father felt displaced in the new neighborhood, while my mom oozed pride. "Not too bad for speaking a little English," my mom would say. "Knowing how to speak English isn't everything."

The move brought about a palpable change of pace. There was a colorfulness to the kinds of immigrants who came into our fish market in Brooklyn that was not present in Queens. The immigrants were of Latino and Slavic descent and seldom came looking for fresh fish. I could feel how sad my father was. He missed the rush of being busy all the time and delivering fresh fish. He began to resent my mother and blamed the slower flow of money on her, verbally and physically.

My brother and I were allowed to hang out around the corner at the nearby post office where we would meet new friends in the neighborhood. The post office became our playground. We hosted our own epic comic book superhero showdowns. Like a troop of monkeys, we swung around the multi-leveled handicap ramp playing Marvel versus DC with our imaginary powers. I was the kid who preyed on the smaller, more defenseless kids because I clearly had not processed my unconscious desire to conquer at that point. This was the same playground where I later decided to assert dominion over a neighbor's German Shepard. I stalked him like a predator while poking and prodding his butt with a stick. When he had enough and took a huge bite into my calf, I limped home to get help. Before taking me to Jamaica Hospital, my mother beat me for making such a careless mistake and for inconveniencing her. Sitting for three hours in the ER waiting for a rabies shot with an over-the-top, shrill Cantonese woman was one of the longest waits of my life.

I had a history of doing the wrong things. In our old Brooklyn apartment, out of spite and jealousy, I ripped the earrings straight out of my sister's newly pierced ears. In a rage, I drew blood from my brother's head by hurling double-D batteries at him when he didn't let me play with his action figures. At a young age, I had so much resentment and anger burning inside of me. It came from my inability to reconcile the actions of my parents. One moment, they would do something loving and supportive, like cooking us delicious, healthy, gourmet meals every day, and in a flash, they would follow that up with an out-of-the-blue harsh reprimand. These polarities paved the way for my inner rebel to blossom.

My fascination with misconduct and the darker sides of things was ongoing. I once uncovered the back of my family's ancestral altar and discovered dozens of baby spiders hatching from their silk nest. I had just read *Charlotte's Web* in school, a children's story about a pig and spider becoming the best of unlikely friends. Apathetically, I took a stick of incense and set the nest on fire. I forced a rapid exodus of newly born spiders out of their mother's protective nest. *If I was able to grow up quickly without warning, then you, my little hatchlings, can do it too. There's no time to dawdle in your complacency.*

One afternoon, I snuck into my neighbor's apartment upstairs and gouged the eyes of all their goldfish with a safety pin. He invited my brother over to play Super Mario Brothers on his Super Nintendo. I apparently wasn't good enough, so I was rejected from their company. All I wanted was to feel included and play. I settled for revenge. I delighted in the way it felt, so I did it a few more times, eventually destroying his entire tank of goldfish. I seared my cat in scalding hot water to see how she would flinch. I used a mallet to bash the brains of flailing snapper fish to bits even well after they were dead. I torturously pried the legs off of living crabs just to see who would win during a two-legged race. No one ever found out.

This apathy was the antithesis to my reaction to the time my father brought me to a live poultry shop and told me to pick out a chicken. I was mortified when they snapped its neck in front of me. There was something about being surrounded by a chorus of live chickens clucking away in fear of their impending doom. The combination of me choosing the chicken, the snapping sound of its neck, and the silence from the flock when one of their own was executed, triggered a surge of guilt within. I suddenly felt a wave of regret for all the acts of cruelty I had committed up until that point, which were essentially acts of misplaced aggression. As a child, I often flew from one extreme to the other. I was not caught up with good and bad for too long. In the back of my mind, I knew that all of my outward transgressions paralleled my parents' authority over me. Naturally, I sought power over whoever or whatever I could. And like a pendulum, I swung from one side to the other, occupying the different shades between light and shadow.

After sentencing a chicken to its gruesome death, I vowed to never eat animals again. But my parents disapproved and once again antagonized me over what they called sentimental idealism. "It is the law of the natural world, and it is our divine right. We are masters over all animals," my dad argued. Over the course of a week, my mom compelled me to eat meat by locking me in the kitchen until I was forced to comply.

Though I fought with my parents incessantly, I empathized with how ostracized they felt every time they experienced discrimination. As blue collar workers who immigrated to America in their thirties, they felt pressured for time. Instead of going to school or spending nearly the amount of time I have been fortunate enough to spend on self-development, they went to work straight away and started a family. They did not have the opportunity to learn English as fluently as they would have liked and depended on me and my siblings to translate. As soon as I could read bills and letters coherently, I was constantly at my father or mother's side defending them. My brother and I took turns, but, ironically, even though I disliked Chinese school, I had better translation skills than he did.

I don't remember the first incident because there were so many scenarios where I had to play the defense attorney. I grudgingly obliged. Most of the time, I was at some bureau disputing an overcharged water or heating bill, or at the DMV defending my father's traffic offenses. If I didn't argue hard enough, my parents took that as me not standing up for them. The one New York quality that my parents did adopt was their capacity to fight the fight. They fought every dispute whether they were right or wrong. Half of the time, they were in the wrong. I wasn't old enough for any government employee to take seriously and felt enormous pressure to prove my loyalty to the family honor. If I succeeded, I got a thankless sigh of relief, and if I failed, my parents blamed me for losing the case. They would interpret my lack of confidence and uncertainty as dispassion for fighting for their cause. It was always a lose-lose situation.

Most of these situations occurred in a public forum, and I could feel the unfavorable looks other people gave my parents. Occasionally, I caught the eye of a Latino or Russian kid doing the same for their parents. So at least I wasn't alone, but still, I would have rather not been put in the situation at all. Before defending any case, I always needed to know from my parents if they were guilty of the accusation. "Were you actually in the wrong?" I would ask. And of course my mom would screech, "What does it matter? You are always standing up for everyone but your own parents. What kind of ungrateful son are you?"

Growing up in Woodhaven, Queens, in the 1990s as an Asian kid was hard. One Halloween, my parents instructed us to stay indoors and, for the first time ever, closed up shop at 3 PM. The Chinese restaurant across the street was one of the few businesses that stayed opened. From our third-story window I watched the events that followed half in horror and half in excitement. Members of a Latino gang marched double file with bats, knives and machetes in hand. They dragged the owner of the restaurant onto the street as his wife cried in protest. He was the father of one of the kids we played with at the post office. They beat and kicked him against the fire hydrant. Then, without warning, one of the gang members took his machete and hacked into the owner's thigh with one swift stroke. The screams from him and his family terrorized me for weeks on end. I was too young to know why they marched into his restaurant and hurt him that way. But I saw this brutal act of aggression as an act against their culture and ours. The fact that dreadful things could happen to me just because I was different was made very real that day. As a result, I withdrew further into my already reserved nature.

We got egged most Halloweens and Fourths of July. Junior high school kids would come in and mock my parents with their derisive "ching ching chong chong" taunts. I suppose the stabbings and the occasional gunshots going off in the distance didn't faze my parents because it was a step up from communist rural China in the '50s and '60s. Occasionally, my father snapped, finding himself in fistfights with instigators who came into our store to shoplift or just knock down a shelf of Asian dry foods for the hell of it. I knew the only way to calm him down was to throw myself in between him and the aggressor. In those moments of heated battle, he was no longer capable of covering up the rage seething through his eyes. He had that desperate yet ferocious look that wild dogs get when dueling over territorial claims. The oppressed animal in him awoke, and he would start fighting for his life like how I imagined he did in the days of his family's persecution. This adolescent version of me who held my feral father back from the many provokers empathized with the emotional scars my father had accumulated.

So, at a young age, I learned that I had to lie sometimes in order to protect the family. Whether I liked it or not, I belonged to a family who was ostracized by American society for their non-White, non-Latino and non-Black background.

At school, we were brainwashed to believe in Walt Disney and fairy-tale endings. I so wanted to believe in the rainbow magic of the American dream, but the truth was that I didn't feel like part of the over-glorified concept of America's Manifest Destiny. We didn't live in Chinatown or Flushing or the Asian part of Brooklyn like most other Asian American families. In Chinatown, I could have lived in a protective bubble speaking Chinese all the time, as if it were a microcosm of China. Instead, I was reminded of my otherness every day walking down Jamaica Avenue.

However, the great benefit to coming to terms with these cultural clashes was that it greatly influenced my ability to arrive at the middle ground between both sides of any story. I concluded that the same kind of abuse my parents suffered during the Cultural Revolution was being mirrored every time they were discriminated against. In China, it was classist; in America, it was racist. Nonetheless, in both scenarios, it was a cyclical story of the abused lashing out. My parents always adopted the spirit of the fighter, and so they always attracted and continue to enter situations where they had to defend themselves. Though I bore witness to my parents' many bouts with cultural and racial intolerance, I didn't suffer as much in those kinds of situations.

By the time I was a teenager, I was influenced by the exciting multidimensionality of characters from American classics—books that nearly all teenagers are forced to read at one point or another: *The Catcher in the Rye, Of Mice and Men, A Tale of Two Cities, The Scarlet Letter*, and *The Adventures of Tom Sawyer*. I immediately identified with the ostracized characters and all the symbolism representing the underdog. This next stage of development in nourishing my inner rebel took on a different tone of me naïvely opposing the establishment of capitalism.

My inner Tom Sawyer and Robin Hood vigilantes took me out on five-finger-discount shopping sprees. It was only at major chains and not mom-and-pop-type shops. I justified taking what I saw as mine from any chain store that I deemed as White America. It was my way of trying to wound the corporate bully that constantly reminded me that I didn't belong. The upside was that I wasn't in a gang. I became the untouchable lone ranger living by my own set of rules on the outskirts of town.

I was an avid atheist and used science to argue the nonexistence of God. The pessimist in me saw things like the creation of Santa Claus as mind control and rigid Christians sugarcoating the miseries of reality. This phase of hating anything to do with the clergy and anything to do with God was etched into me when my parents sublet one of our rooms to a man from northern China one year.

I liked going into his room because my parents told me not to. I would sit in a cloud of cigarette smoke as he told me stories about the beauty of communism and how capitalism was the weapon of Western imperialism. Most of the things he talked about went way over my head as he spoke partly in Mandarin (which I don't speak) and broken English. I absorbed 40 percent of what he told me and nodded anytime his pirate-like accent made it too hard to make the connection between Mandarin and Cantonese. What was most memorable was the essence of what he was trying to impart. One of them was the Marxist ideal that religion is the opiate of the masses.

It was liberating to see this man on the fringes of society living a truth contrary to my father's views on communism. It gave me the strength to see that I didn't have to do exactly what my parents wanted. I could be like our chain-smoking anti-capitalist tenant who marched to the beat of his own drum.

He only stayed with us for a few months. I was fond of this odd character who made a cameo appearance in my adolescent years. He gave me more confidence to question and doubt the status quo. He helped me do my calligraphy homework and gave me a book in Chinese to read about the conspiracy of the Opium War. If Google

Translate were around those days, I might have made it past the introduction. Trying to translate a language with no alphabet to a language with an alphabet was entirely too draining.

He definitely encouraged me to embrace the part of me that was the devil's advocate. This played out brilliantly during debates in school. My high school was famous for its school-wide mock simulation of the elections. During my senior year, it was the New York State gubernatorial election with George Pataki on the Republican ticket, and the first-ever elected African-American state comptroller, Carl McCall, as the Democratic opponent. Every person was assigned a role to play that mirrored the actual elections. My class was assigned to play the Democrats, and I somehow was voted to play Carl McCall. My overachieving self was ready to take the limelight and stand up on stage during all of the debates and destroy the competition.

In the actual election, McCall lost to Pataki with only 33 percent of the vote, a surprisingly low number for a state that normally votes blue. And in my school simulation, I won with a whopping 70 percent landslide. I remember blowing social and environmental concerns way out of proportion and spinning them in my favor, even though in real life the issues argued were different and McCall was losing badly. I clawed my nails into a sensitive post-9/11 sentiment by harping on how Pataki's Indian Point nuclear power plant was a terrorist attack and environmental disaster waiting to happen. If there was anything I learned from my Chinese pirate friend, it was that everyone would believe me so long as I was emotionally committed to my message. I was taking issues and adding my own impassioned opinions to make a stand. My school voted for me because they believed that I believed very strongly about what I represented.

My spiritual teacher, Swami Amitanand, later reinforced this idea. He said that beliefs were like clothes. Some people like to wear the same clothes every day, and some keep changing them like every week is Fashion Week. When we have a group of people wearing similar clothes, a culture of like-minded individuals is created. In high school, my truth was that I believed in the values of Robin Hood and protecting the common man, and it showed through any assignment I was doing. I was always in search of those with the same values as myself, going so far as to convince others to believe in what I believed.

Belief will always be an external force trying to create influence. However, only the truth can be verified through a confirmed experience of the matter at hand. If our experiences disprove a previously-thought-true belief system, then that belief system doesn't matter anymore. Experience always supersedes belief, whether we like it or not. So, if the belief is that nuclear power plants have the potential for mass destruction, the experience of witnessing Chernobyl secondhand through videos and hearing the stories of the survivors would confirm that belief true. If, all of a sudden, someone discovered a way to turn nuclear power plants into the safest and most efficient way of producing energy, a new belief system would be introduced, and only experience could validate it (in this case, cold hard scientific facts would have to be produced). If we choose to continue to believe in something that has been disproved by our own experiences, then we might as well join the ranks of fanatical zealots in denial. Hence, my favorite saying, which all my spiritual teachers have in common, is "You cannot unsee what you have seen."

For example, as I deepened my martial arts practice and became more sensitive to energy, I gradually redefined myself as a softened agnostic instead of an ardent atheist. By the time yoga made its way into my life at twenty, I was chanting Sanskrit at community kirtans (devotional chanting circles) and thirsty for any spiritual teacher that could help shed some light on the meaning of life and the purpose of my soul. The yoga movement to me felt like a provocative rebellion that went against the grain. Teachers preached against the soul suckers of corporate America and animal cruelty, offering a fresh perspective on how to see the world. I finally found a tribe I wanted to willingly join.

I bounced around with the bhakti yogis, chanting my heart out, going to the Siddha yogis in midtown and receiving the blessings of Amma, the Indian hugging saint, when she came into town. I gravitated to many different healing modalities on my quest for myself, and discovered a whole new world of possibilities. It was refreshing.

In order to fully make a choice about what to believe or not to believe, I had to live each phase until it played itself out. In my twenties, I was addicted to finding answers. It was a period of insatiable seeking. I fell in love with the peaceful denouement of a sweaty yoga class, just as much as I got addicted to the high from ecstatically chanting Sanskrit mantras. On the flip side, I was also attached the numbness and wild spontaneity of partying, drinking and drugs.

I attribute my wildness to being conditioned by Hollywood's constant reinforcement of the coming-of-age story. With a generation of movies in the genre of *Can't Hardly Wait* and *American Pie*, there was this tangible, collective pressure to party hard until I was stupid in the head. My abstinent high school years of resisting temptation and avoiding people put me in a fantasy world where I used my imagination to escape. This all exploded in college when I went through five years of self-discovery and freedom of expression.

My parents would never have given me free rein to make the mistake of doing drugs. With countless stories of cousins and other family members overdosing on heroin in Hong Kong or getting involved with gangs, staying away from drugs was pounded into our minds. As far as our parents were concerned, if we so much as tried cigarettes, we were criminals in a gang. My parents even affiliated men with tattoos and long hair with scum of the earth. The understanding was that insubordination to my parents' moral code meant an absolute premature death. As often as I provoked my parents with my words, I never crossed that line when it came to drugs for the fear of no return.

When I moved away from home and the harsh restrictions of parental authority were nowhere in sight, I went to frat parties and crossed those boundaries. I picked up a fake ID, flew to New Orleans for my first spring break, and partied so hard that I don't remember much of the trip anymore. Growing up, my parents were too frugal for family bonding, so this was my first time on a plane. It was a week of many firsts. It was my first experience in the South. I saw palm trees for the first time. I lost my virginity to a complete stranger. It was my first time visiting a strip joint. I was surrounded by so many shady characters and it was liberating. I felt this raw spontaneity as freedom. And in many ways, it was.

Some would liken that to me "getting it out of my system." I object to this puritanical phrase because it automatically implies that there is a better or worse way of existing. The same curiosity that sparked my wanting to experience different shades of my darkness led me to draw blood from my brother and sister when I was a child.

Whether it was right or wrong, I needed to experience my choices on my own accord and understand the consequences for the sake of knowing myself as authentically as I could. It was important to have the freedom to make my own mistakes. Over time, I've learned that these shadow aspects of me can never be destroyed. They will always be there. Today they are kept at bay not because I've repressed them, but because I understand them. In acknowledging them, I have learned that all of the various archetypes of self I have embodied sought to protect me. After becoming aware of that, they hold less influence over me.

Some people visualize the lifestyle of a yogi or spiritual teacher as one confined to monastic abstinence from all worldly cravings. Though the monastic orders of the world are valid paths, it is not how I envision the majority of the world awakening to a new path of spirituality. Some people need a lot of structure and are drawn to the strictness of rules to attain self-realization, while spirituality for me consists of a fluid ability to make choices without regret—to experience the richness of life in all its flavors without becoming addicted to pleasure and pain.

When we don't do something because society tells us it is wrong, we deny ourselves from a place of fear. It may be a collective fear of addiction or pain, or whatever the story may be. But the point is that the "don't do this, or else" mentality is a fear paradigm. Unfortunately, that leads us down the path of emotional repression. I have met plenty of people who would rather live in the bounds of what is perceived as "good" than step one foot into the realm of the "bad"—for fear of what their parents may think, for fear of not belonging, or for fear of the unfamiliar.

The fear list has so many variations, but in essence it all boils down to everyone having the universal fear of rejection, the fear of the unknown, the fear of death, literally and figuratively. In the *Yoga Sutras*, Patanjali talks about the five *kleshas*, which are the five roots of pain and suffering: *avidya*—ignorance; *asmita*—ego; *raga*—attachments; *dvesa*—aversions; *abhinivesha*—fear of death. For me, the fear of dying has been most limiting in my spiritual evolution.

Through my somatic awareness training, it was easy for me to understand that my obstacles were always rooted in egotistical attachment and/or aversion. Ultimately, the fear of crossing the border into the realm where nothing would ever be the same again was always the most challenging for me. It meant leaving a world of old friends, comfort and familiarity behind. It meant burning the old stories that kept me stuck in sameness. Only when they were released would I rise anew like the phoenix from the ash.

When I was twenty-four studying in India, my spiritual teacher, Swami Amitanand, told me about a Greek-Russian mystic named Gurdjieff. He was highly unorthodox in his human development methods. One of the ways Gurdjieff helped people with their issues, whether health or spirit related, was to require them to become intoxicated under the influence of psychoactive substances, alcohol, opium, or hashish so that he could observe their behaviors. If someone objected to his madness, he would not work with them. The purpose was to see who they were concealing under the mask they wore on a daily basis.

We have all experienced this unmasking when we have a night on the town and see our introspective friends turn into messy, larger-than-life personalities, and vice versa. In my early inebriated states, I often became melancholic. It was very illuminating to be repeatedly made aware of my patterns of self-sabotage and self-destruction, which were almost always based on this deep desire to feel loved and like I belonged to a tribe of those who got me.

Gurdjieff's main change agent was the conscious use of alcohol. He claimed that it brought the neuroses and the essence of the person into the light. He went on to explain that

> . . . in a man . . . two beings, as it were, are formed in him, who speak in different voices, have completely different tastes, aims and interests, and one of these two beings often proves to be on the level of a small child . . . Certain narcotics have the property of putting personality to sleep without affecting essence. And for a certain time after taking this narcotic a man's personality disappears, as it were, and only his essence remains."[2]

---

2   P. D. Ouspensky, *In Search of the Miraculous: Fragments of an Unknown Teaching* (New York: Harcourt, Brace & World, 1949, p 162)

He boldly dubbed his way of self-development as the "The Fourth Way," and much to my astonishment, he showed a similar understanding of the mind, body and emotions that I have come to realize for myself. I love the *Yoga Sutras*, but I found the tenets of what to do, and what not to do, very cerebral. Though in its pure essence the whole of yoga promotes the integration of the mind, body and emotions, while the sutras focus on the mind as the main vehicle to affect this change. I could not help but feel sometimes that yoga leads to a compartmentalized life versus a more integrative and nonlinear approach.

Gurdjieff said his Fourth Way integrated the three other paths, the way of the fakir (body based), the way of the monk (feeling based) and the way of the yogi (mind based). It didn't require a commitment to make drastic sacrifices or follow a saint or guru. His awakening process was a series of experiences that brought all the different energetic systems into wholeness. In an interview with *The New York Times*, Madame de Salzmann, who studied from Gurdjieff himself, said

> You see, one's thought and body are never in touch with each other, and when these centers are finally linked, one receives impressions through the whole person and not just through a part of oneself.[3]

I was most struck by my spiritual teacher Swami Amitanand's explanation of how Gurdjieff worked with someone with anger management issues. He encouraged a full expression of the emotion of anger while developing an intimate relationship with it. This relationship becomes an elevated awareness over time. He taught people to experience anger while becoming aware of it as a witness simultaneously. Then the emotion of anger can run its course without us creating attachments to the drama. It was very much like an actor learning to distinguish himself from the character and the play he is in. And in that experience of witnessing, we un-identify with the action of doing and elevate to a higher state of conscious being.

---

3   *The New York Times*, "Getting in Touch with Gurdjieff," Margaret Croydon, July 29, 1979

I learned about Gurdjieff in India, and loved his unorthodox methods. His outright rebellion against the accepted, traditional spiritual teachings resonated so deeply with me. All the guilt I had about my wild early twenties evaporated. And being that most of my choices were governed by a raw, unfiltered anger at my parents, society, the world and myself, I was encouraged to embrace my anger. I had to get very acquainted with this force in order to transform it. There was no sense in trying to repress this powerful force. My emotional blueprint defaults to anger. I don't know why. It just does. We don't question why a tiger is a tiger, or why a snake strikes the way it does. It just is, and we accept it.

So, instead of wishing to never feel anger again, or entertaining anger through complaining and frustration, I had the potential to rechannel anger into passion. All the indignation and frustration I felt at how the status quo was telling me to live my life was more useful as motivation than as an outburst. And this could only happen when I understood that healing myself was not about compartmentalizing desirable sensations into a file labeled *Good* and undesirable sensations into another file labeled *Bad*.

I had to rewire my brain to disassociate from the conditioned value judgments of what was socially acceptable in terms of the moral compass. It no longer made sense to strive to be "the good guy" or "the bad guy." I have since shed these labels and made concrete decisions in my life with discernment. In doing so, guilt was naturally deleted from my library of useful feelings. If I do feel guilt on the rare occasion, I reevaluate its true origin. Most likely, it comes from an unfair expectation I unknowingly or knowingly placed on myself. Once those expectations are removed, guilt disappears and has no more power over me. I cannot manage how others think of me, nor manage the expectations of others, but I can manage my expectations for myself.

Channeling the inner rebel really is about breaking this vicious cycle of guilt. Life becomes so much more colorful and purposeful when we can hack into the programming that keeps us in this limited framework. The hardest part is realizing that we hold the control switch to either keep running our outdated programming or completely reconstruct it into something unrecognizable and brand new.

Funnily enough, I trained as an actor, who is a rebel by nature. And it was not until acting school ended that I realized the amazing honor and privilege of my training and how crucial it was in my spiritual development. I suppose it was the universe's plan for me all along. Everything I did as a child was consistent in challenging the status quo. That evolved into mirroring the human experience from the stage to the audience with the purpose of inspiring self-discovery. I have had the great opportunity of expressing a large range in the spectrum of my humanness as an outright rebellion to the forces that seek to limit and confine us. It is my wish that we all connect with our inner rebel and reclaim our birthright to experience the infinite possibilities at our fingertips.

CHAPTER 8

EMBRACING SPIRITUALITY THROUGH MATERIALISM

ॐ

"Never create any antagonism between materialism and spiritualism—they go together; just as body and soul. Remain materialistic and use your materialism as a stepping-stone towards spirituality."

OSHO

If I had to identify when I healed from the deep-seated issues of my psyche as defined by the four archetypes, I wouldn't be able to clearly delineate a time and date when one was fully resolved. The learnings are ongoing, and I am not so caught up with whether or not I am done with resolving an issue as I am in enjoying the bumpy ride. And in this way, the healing process is a series of realizations over time that culminate in a deep internal shift. Some are spontaneous and quick, like the time the sky split open at SUNY Geneseo, while others are co-created with the universe over time. Deep down, I believe my soul was fed up with lifetimes of emotionally masturbating through the same issues over and over again. And one of my biggest breakthroughs on the spiritual path was learning to not suppress my drive to succeed. I had to learn to be okay with wanting money.

For that to happen, a massive shift in my consciousness was needed. I unconsciously associated monetary wealth with greedy egomaniacs. The Robin Hood anti-capitalist mindset from my youth was present throughout the beginnings of my spiritual path. I was torn between the easygoing day-by-day attitude of the frugal traveler and honoring that part of myself that is fond of the luxurious things in life.

My parents spent most of their life saving up to buy their own home. Everything was about penny-pinching and repressing any enjoyment in life. No family holidays because they were a waste of money. No fancy clothes because that would be excessive. Everything purchased in our house, no matter how small, was considered an investment, and the value had to be carefully weighed before making a decision.

Chinese New Year was a time of strategic planning when my parents visited family friends. Culturally, children awaited this holiday with a greedy expectancy because married people were supposed to gift children with red envelopes of cash for good luck and for warding off evil spirits. For me, it was a time of playing a game of prediction with myself. I guessed which family we would visit next. We always seemed to visit the families with one or two kids. We were three, so if we had generous envelopes, then my parents made a profit. Unlike other kids who kept their New Year's money to top up their allowance, I knew mine needed to be recycled to our parents so they could repackage it.

I started working for minimum wage at five dollars an hour at the age of fourteen, helping to look after kids in a summer school program, and had worked hard to save my money since then. From an early age, I scrimped. Most altercations between my parents were about money. They would literally get into fistfights and throw each other across the room because of it. Ultimately, my wariness of spending too much developed into an unhealthy fear of not having enough. Not enough money, not enough food, not enough affection, not enough attention, not enough support, not enough friends, not enough smarts, not enough love.

I thought that the universe had a finite amount of resources to give me and it was nickel-and-diming how much to divvy up to the citizens of earth. Even though I strived to fall as far from the apple tree as I could, the imprint of scarcity from my parents' traumatic confrontation with communism trickled down into my belief systems.

I spent many years grappling with the concept of abundance. The issue went hand in hand with my self-worth. *How much do I value myself? Am I even worthy of this?* Even when I was managing Studio Anya in New York, creating programs and co-facilitating teacher training programs with Courtney, I was struggling with it. It was so difficult to ask for money from clients. This seemed to be a running theme among the movement teachers. We had this agreement to collect the tuition fees for each other's private clients. We even had a group discussion once about how uncomfortable it felt to ask our clients to top up their packages because it felt like we were disturbing the friendship that would inevitably form with them over time. Why did it feel wrong to ask for money for our expertise and time? Why did it feel wrong to ask for money to pay the rent and put food in our mouths?

In the three different yoga teacher training programs that I attended, the paradox of spirituality and business always came up. Those who were most vocal about it always expressed the opinion that if we were truly spiritual, then all self-development classes like yoga or meditation should be nearly free. "It's too expensive, so it can't be authentic; it can't be spiritual" seemed to be the conclusion.

At the end of the day, it was up to me to discern the difference between what was true and not true for me. I had to ask some serious questions to reconcile the discord between spirituality and materialism. Were these opinions about money based on a fear of scarcity? Were we criticizing the value of money because of the countless political scandals and government corruption stories that we are inundated with by the media? Why was I afraid of asking for money?

One useful tool I can impart on how I made peace with this issue is the practice of *viveka*, the yogic concept of discernment. When we zoom into the essence of what discernment really is, we see that it's an upgrade of our capacity to pass judgment. It is the ability to distinguish what is real and what is not real by connecting to our heart's truth. All of these notions about money and the evilness of money that I learned from society at large were fear-based programs designed to keep me small-minded. And these programs fed my inner saboteur. With a lot of contemplation, I redefined my relationship with money. I did not even need to learn how to ask for money for my services in a guilt-free way. I simply had to dismantle these outdated lack-based programs; then, asking for money was not clouded by old layers of lies.

One difference between the spiritual seeker I was in my twenties and the seeker I am in my thirties is the powerful and simple practice of *viveka*. I no longer feel the desire to uncover the "whys" of everything. I no longer feel pressure to find all the answers. Through discernment, I've learned to trust my internal compass; so, come what may, I will remain unattached to the end result. Spirituality is no longer a manic search for what is right and wrong, but rather a process of living the questions daily.

A big test of discernment came during my Christmas break at the end of 2017 when I visited Pune, India, for two weeks. My spiritual teacher Swami Amitanand (I call him Swamiji for short) in Rishikesh is an Osho sannyasi and bestowed upon me the spiritual name of Anand Saurabh in 2011, which inherently associated me with the Osho lineage. At one point, he encouraged me to visit the Osho Meditation Resort, where he once lived and studied under the Indian mystic Rajneesh Osho in the late 1980s when it was still an ashram. Osho preached integrating the lifestyle of the Greek materialist, Zorba, with the spiritual wisdom of the Buddha. He taught that everyone had the choice of receiving spiritual and material wealth without sacrificing one over the other.

I always wanted to stay at the Osho Meditation Resort when I visited India during my twenties, but I was never able to afford the rates. Fast-forward a decade to me owning my own business - I finally was able to do it.

My partner, Andy, was itching to rent a camper van and drive through New Zealand. After an intense year of giving birth to my newly opened studio, Sagehouse in Singapore, my intuition guided me to rest and restore. A short five-hour flight to Mumbai and four hours of driving to Pune landed us in the Conrad hotel a kilometer away from the Osho center. Over the years, I've learned to discern the truth behind the different voices in my head and follow the one voice that serves my highest benefit. That voice guided me to not stay within the compound, even though my ego wanted to check a full immersion at the Osho center off my bucket list. Ego said anything less than staying inside the compound was not deemed worthy enough and would not be as spiritually credible. But I knew that it wasn't what I needed.

The practice of discernment is the practice of choosing what brings our highest benefit physically, mentally, emotionally and spiritually without attaching to a projected outcome. After some back and forth, we ended up staying at the Conrad, which became a luxurious cave for me to contemplate and journal. The spiritual egomaniac in me saw my time in Pune as adding more credentials to my resume. Ultimately, I took heed of destiny and started a new chapter in my personal development and service to humanity by starting the beginnings of this book.

Deep down, I already knew I did not need an immersive experience in the Osho work, though it would have been nice to practice it in a large group. With Swami Amitanand in Rishikesh years back during my Reiki master training, I had practiced the major transformative meditations, like the dynamic meditation, kundalini and the Nadabrahma along with whirling, Nataraj and No Dimension. It was done one-on-one under Swamiji's guidance, and the energetic shifts I felt under such an adept master were entirely different from the diluted experience of doing it en masse led by a group of spiritual volunteers. I became absolutely enthralled with Osho's discourses and thirstily read as many of his books as I could find. I was so excited to step foot on such adored ground.

Osho created so many different types of active meditations, all with the intention of getting the modern man out of his neurotic, overthinking mind and into the body and soul. Why live a one-note life through our mental faculties when we are so much more? Swamiji guided me through the main meditations that he felt served my spiritual evolution. And after coming out on the other side of that ring of fire, I was more aligned to my authentic true nature than I had ever been before. When I was actually at Osho's main headquarters, my old self thought I would be a little more starstruck or reverent, but

I was not. I realized that the blind idolization of any spiritual teacher, regardless of respect for their teachings, was not the way to go.

I had mixed feelings about being among Osho followers because I never fully identified myself as one. During the evenings, we participated in a group celebratory meeting and meditation and watched Osho talk from the grave on a large video projector. One evening we focused intently as he spoke about the concept of respect. He challenged the traditional concepts of granting unearned respect to elders instead of honoring the purity of youth.

> No society in the world has been, up to now, respectful to the children. All respect is for the elders, all respect is for the old, almost dead. All respect is for the graveyards—no respect for the cradles. And the child is the purest life—uncontaminated. The child is closer to the very source of life than the old man. The old man is closer to death . . . but strange— death has been worshipped, respected, and life has been crushed, destroyed in every possible way.

I recalled that these were some of the first words I read of his which resonated deeply in my bones.

I always wondered why my parents and the older people who surrounded me as a child punished me for my inquisitive nature. They always sought to transform me into an obedient automaton. We learned a Chinese phrase as children: to respect our mother as the earth and our father as the sky. Yet the earth and the sky never sought to restrain my freedom. One day I spoke out against my mother's perpetual use of this phrase in her scolding of me. She demanded respect, and to her and my surprise, I countered with a demand for *her* respect of me. As soon as I blurted that out, I thought the earth would split open and swallow me whole. How dare I even suggest this heretical concept? She raged that I didn't deserve respect and pulled one of my belts from the closet to take her frustrations out on me. She had a surprising amount of strength for such a little woman.

I had similar thoughts when I walked through the admissions office of the Osho Meditation Center. *Am I supposed to blindly kowtow to the home of the teacher of my teacher?* I was greeted by older Osho work-study volunteers. They frequented the center yearly or bi-annually to take part in a work-study program on campus. There was a lack of warmth and hospitality in their eyes and the way they carried themselves. Andy and I did not feel embraced by the spiritual community at all. Was all this meditating supposed to yield a cold exterior? There was a wash of frigidity in a majority of the people we encountered. And I found the many rules and regulations put into practice served the center and not the seekers. Everything from the ration cards and the way they sold food items and meditation clothing, cushions, chairs and the like to the security guard outposts at each major entrance created the air of Big Brother watching us. I was also dubious of the stringent rule where if you coughed in the meditation pyramid during the silent parts of the session, you had to immediately leave, or else you would be escorted out. They explained that Osho made a big deal about preserving the collective silence. I don't doubt that. Nonetheless, the militant enforcement of the rule was curious to me.

Again, I found myself conflicted between authority and respect; this time it was between me and the establishment. It was a practice of politeness, which at times felt like a social pressure. So discernment became the executive decision-maker. *Do I actively speak up and question, or as a guest politely acquiesce?* There was such an eclectic mix of people walking around, from those with a wall of don't-bother-me to the hugging lovey-dovey type, with a higher percentage of the former. I would have much preferred the latter, but I knew firsthand that when people are put into uncomfortable environments for the purpose of deep transformation, it doesn't look like unicorns and rainbows. It's like walking around the aftermath of an old battlefield where open wounds are slowly repairing.

I wondered if this was in alignment with Osho's vision—people leaving meditation class with a standoffish, resting-bitch face comparable to stone. Osho always preached that life is a celebration. But then again, I had to remember that everyone was in their own individual process. All the chaotic dancing and breathing was designed to create an environment to break down conditioned habits and patterns. And as it is with all personal development work, sometimes it gets worse before it gets better, so maybe resting-bitch face was a way to cope. I wonder if I walked around with a resting-bitch face, too.

After all the controversy and political drama surrounding Osho's alleged poisoning on the grounds by his senior disciples, I could not help questioning the authenticity of the environment which was supposed to be nurturing the flock. Rumors, like myths, always have some basis in truth; otherwise they would not exist. And even if the allegations were not true, the energy of these rumors weighed heavily on me. I scrutinized the corporate entity run by these corporate spiritualists who enshrouded the Osho center in a cloud of conjecture. Was the stringent external environment preventing clarity in the collective internal environment?

Whatever it was, I had to trust that everyone was exactly where they needed to be and stop worrying about them and turn my attention to myself. After all, I was there to recalibrate. Yet I could not help but reevaluate my concept of spirituality and materiality. Here I was attending meditation classes on a commune that was worth Rs. 1,500 crore, or approximately 220 million USD, where my spiritual teacher's teacher was rumored to have been murdered. The exact motivations for the murder were unclear, but they were undeniably based in greed. It was no secret that world viewed Osho's collection of 93 Rolls Royces and his flying around on private jets as controversial. Could spirituality be flaunted with such an exorbitant show of wealth?

I had many observations about the overall energy of the establishment and vented a lot to Swamiji over the phone. Even though he shared similar views, he finally dismissed it all with a light chuckle and reminded me that it was all part of the game of life, and to not get so easily absorbed in the gossip and drama. Osho defenders have said that most of his wealth was donated to him by followers, and that he eventually gave most of it away. They have also said it was his way of mirroring the ridiculousness of American consumerism.

We will never really know exactly what transpired during the dark days surrounding his death. The important thing to learn from his revolutionary concepts of material spirituality is that there is a fine line that needs constant attention. Checks and balances rooted in the ability to discern when the ego is overriding the authenticity of the heart need to be vigilantly maintained. Even the current accusations of the Osho Trust committing fraud and illegal reappropriation of money provide a spiritual lesson—on the dangers of collapsing into greed and ego.

After my conversations with Swamiji, I was reminded to find humor in it all. Like Shakespeare says, life really is a stage, and we are actors playing our parts, so why not be less serious and more playful about it? It's not like I signed up for enlightenment camp with the guarantee of transcending reality at the end of two weeks. I had come to experience, without expectation, the light and the dark.

Once I let go of the titillating Osho drama, I refocused on the task at hand. I had come to do my own yoga practice in the morning followed by a half day of meditation to reconnect with my creativity and to recharge my batteries. I had to let go of rational thought, judgments of people, and opinions in order to receive with openness the visions and sensations that soon flowed through my entire being. The tricky part was then articulating those sensations through the keyboard.

Everyone gathered hourly in the meditation pyramid, which to date is the largest meditation hall in the world. The daily program included multiple active meditations, with ongoing meditation and experiential workshops designed to connect us to our higher selves. The purity of Osho's meditations was maintained by being taught via video recordings and monitored by facilitators. My sense of the meditations was much more neutral than I remembered feeling in Rishikesh, I suppose because I was more adept at accessing a meditative state quickly, and I was not the same person as I was during my fledgling years of seeking. This time around, the meditations served mainly as a portal for me to access my creativity more deeply while at the same time transmuting emotional and karmic residue stuck in my mind and body. In the past, my experiences were more fixated on the latter.

In Swamiji's meditation room in Rishikesh, he blindfolded me and invited me to practice these active meditations daily followed by a Reiki intensive for two to three hours a day. At the time, the Osho meditations helped to clear the emotions that were repressed in my body. I was instructed to go into *mauna*, or "prolonged silence," where I would not talk for four days. This was nothing compared to what he had done when he was in residence at the Maharishi ashram— silence for twenty-one days with only water to drink under the strict confinement of a meditation dome that served as his humble quarters. He explained that the movement of energy in our current time had quickened, and through most of the clearing practices I had already done, it was not necessary to do such a long *mauna*. All the processes were moving at an exponentially faster speed. He told me not to compare my journey with his. It was of a different time, place and energy. That he endured longer periods of silence should not prompt me to try it in an attempt to prove my worthiness. In short, he had put me on the fast track because humanity was running out of time, and I didn't have the luxury of sitting in cave for ten years to then come out and share realized wisdom with the world.

The active meditations involved wild jumping, dancing, chaotic shaking and rapid breathing. It was physically exhausting but energetically invigorating. It broke me out of linear thinking, doubting and fearing, and into learning how to feel in the present moment. Swamiji reminded me over and over again that these meditations were just tools, and that meditation is a state of being and not doing. These tools entrain a state of perpetual meditation in our waking state without having to work so hard to get there. The active meditations are the equivalent of rehearsals, and the actual state of meditation is the live performance, which is living life.

Immediately after my sessions with Swamiji, there was a sense of stillness and quiet in my mind, but an hour or two afterward, on my own, I sometimes cried incessantly, feeling emotionally overwhelmed. My mood swings were unpredictable and unexpected. It was part of cleaning the dirty cobwebs out of my attic and basement that I had ignored for years.

During my stay at the Osho center, I witnessed many seekers in this stage of self-exploration—a vulnerable state that I knew all too well. The seekers enrolled in the silent program looked miserable. They were going through a deep emotional battle unique to themselves. One of them even lashed out and reprimanded me and Andy for mistakenly sitting at the silent table in the dining area. Other seekers looked disheveled and ungrounded from reality, just as I had been half a decade earlier. It was a reminder that if meditation is not applied in the here and now, it simply becomes another form of avoidance, a type of head-in-the-clouds, airy fairy escapism.

If I had chosen to stay within the compound, I would have

been sucked up into a totally different experience. The freedom to leave allowed me to focus on the mission at hand: channeling my creative energies into writing something that would be relatable to the modern-day urban seeker.

My lesson this time around was not one of inner peace. I had already embraced the vibrant chaos within, and inner peace was really just coming to terms with that chaos. I had already learned to embrace the ups and downs of my mood swings. Like the changing of the tide, my emotions needed to run their course to prevent a catastrophic eruption. My lesson this time around was about embracing my dharma, or my path.

And that path isn't a passive path hidden in a cave retreat. I was designed as a bridge between the material and spiritual. And by design, I declare the age-old battle between money and the spirit to be outdated. True spirituality rises above the dualistic notions of right and wrong or good and bad. The key to humanity's awakening of consciousness rests not in how well we continue existing in our compartmentalized lives but on how well the world redefines the relationship between what we perceive as sacred and what is not sacred.

CHAPTER 9

TRIP TO INDIA: THE VIRGIN VOYAGE ON A QUEST FOR WHO I AM

"Mother India is in many ways the mother of us all."

WILLIAM DURANT

My inner peace was a hard lesson to grasp. This elusive holy grail of self-mastery eventually came, but not without a thorough and repetitive internal cleaning and scrubbing of all my conditioned patterns of operating. It's still a work in progress. At the very least, I am now aware of the way I swing from one end of the spectrum to the other. And a lot of this awareness was developed during my virgin voyage to the unforgettable motherland: India.

September 2011, this phase of searching for inner peace required me to leave everything I knew to journey to the birthplace of yoga, which I perceived as a magical place holding all the answers. In a presumptuous manner that was still tied to the old way of compartmentalized being, I gave myself three months to find it. I liked to give myself deadlines. They were milestones to keep me on track. When the decision was made, I enrolled in my advanced 500-hour yoga teacher training with Yogirishi Vishvaketu, the founder of Akhanda Yoga and yoga guru of Anand Prakash Ashram. I had always wanted to study yoga in India, and he kept appearing in my internet searches. I took it as a digital sign from the universe and happily penciled my second yoga teacher training into my self-imposed timeline of finding peace within.

Those three months were timeless. It could have been three years. Time didn't function in the same kind of hurry as it did in New York. And the way I felt things was amplified in a way I had never experienced before. It was as if the wind sang a warm welcome when I first set foot on the Himalayan foothills. I instantly felt a deep connection with the land as if I were home again—like a bullet train through the railway of my spine, or like light bulbs switched off for a long time had suddenly switched on. My mind, body and spirit were ripe after four years of actor training. I began the express journey of acknowledging and embracing all the conditioned patterns and behaviors that I knowingly and unknowingly collected over the years. At the time, I didn't know this trip would catalyze the next phase of my spiritual development.

In the summer of 2011, I was in my then-longest relationship of my life, a whopping eight months. It was the most forced and incompatible match ever made. Mentally, emotionally and soul-wise, we were not on the same page, but I dragged it on in my attempt to feel loved and needed. The one benefit that came from the relationship was that my ex encouraged me to come out to my parents.

After we broke up, I performed a reading using a Native American animal totem deck to ease the pangs of heartbreak. I was shown a spread of animal guides revealing a story around the blue heron. The spread showed that he was meant to fly in and fly out of my life for one purpose only. He was like the fabled stork who brings life and then disappears. In the end, he served as a major catalyst during an awkward period of my life. Then, he passed from my memory like rainwater through my fingers.

Before I went to India, I came out to my parents in the only way I was able to: a handwritten letter. I spent hours grudgingly recalling my rusty Chinese. I had the help of an online dictionary to craft the message. Though my parents were American citizens, they only learned enough English to get by on a day-to-day basis and to pass the citizenship exam. There was no way to express myself in my preferred tongue, English. I felt more expressive in Spanish than I did in Cantonese. It was agony to try and express myself in a language and culture that I felt rejected and attacked for so many years.

When I was a little kid, I vowed that I would keep my parents in the dark forever. By the time I was a teenager, I conjectured maybe the age of thirty-five or forty would be a good time to come out. But, deep down, I knew I could no longer afford to wait in shattering their expectations of who they wanted me to be. It was gnawing at me. Working in the gayest restaurant in Chelsea, Elmo, and being surrounded by so many gay people who were so unabashedly open about who they were also rubbed off on me. What had seemed like a distant reality for me was coming to life sooner than I anticipated. In the back of my mind, I made excuses that these liberated gays didn't understand my conservative parents and my rigid culture. They didn't understand what I had to go through. Despite my limiting beliefs, my higher self won. At twenty-six, I wrote a letter, dumped it in the mailbox, and jumped on a plane to India for three months with my big, gay, tangerine-colored Ralph Lauren suitcase.

The first week I was there, I was too overwhelmed with the sights and the sounds to even remember sending the letter. When I landed, I waited for my yogi friend's cousin to pick me up. Needless to say, my first lesson in India was that you should tell someone to pick you up four hours before your actual arrival time. On one hand, there is punctuality, and then on the other hand, there is India time.

I was exhausted by the time I was dropped off 500 meters from my guesthouse. I couldn't be dropped off any closer because the traffic was out of this world. I opted to walk through a colorful street of festive celebration. Unbeknownst to me, I had landed in New Delhi during the holiday of Diwali. The festival of lights. The cacophonous chanting in the temples enhanced the procession of bright saris flooding the streets. Diwali celebrates the triumph of good over evil. And everybody was out. It made a New York subway platform in a sweaty, humid August seem like a cakewalk. The sheer volume of human bodies moving in chaotic harmony was mindboggling. I held onto my belongings tightly as mischievous monkeys swung from electrical cables taking food and anything that glittered. As I stepped out to cross the street to my hostel, a massive ceremonial elephant appeared from the apex of the hill and plowed through the street traffic of cars, cows and chickens.

Encountering the indescribable filth of New Delhi amidst the vibrant flurry of culture was jarring to my unaccustomed eyes and ears. My arrival at a more subdued Rishikesh couldn't come soon enough. I didn't leave New York City to substitute it with more urban chaos. I longed to step foot in the land of the seers and walk the path of the yogi. I dreamed about visiting the infamous home of Maharishi Mahesh Yogi's ashram that inspired the Beatles to meditate and write their songs. I was so close. Just a couple of days in Delhi, and I would be on my way.

After weaving through the crowd and arriving at my guesthouse, I put my things down and ventured out, desperate for a massage parlor. I found an Ayurvedic massage place nearby and eagerly walked in. After all, Ayurveda was the sister of yoga, and I thought I should get more acquainted with what it was about. Plus, it was literally around the corner and my body was destroyed from the bumpy Air India flight.

My male masseur told me to strip completely naked and lie facing up, minus the towel. In spite of my culture shock, I chalked it up to it being the Indian way. Being tired and disoriented, I resigned myself to this new experience. I just wanted to lie down. At the corner of the room was the wooden steam box with a hole for the head. I learned about it on some travel program in Southeast Asia. I assumed it made sense that one would be naked for massage before a full body steam. So I went with it. I had a male masseur and thought nothing of it. It took me a few moments to realize that I was not in the most reputable of establishments.

My entire arrival was just a shock to my system. I didn't make a big deal of it; I was too tired. I unplugged from the craziness of a massive misunderstanding, went back to the guesthouse and went to sleep. The next day, I did some touristy things that I can't even recall and later that evening met up with my friend's cousin again, who introduced me to his gang of friends. They hung out on the stoop of one city block, shouting and jeering at people they seemed to know. I didn't know what they were yelling about, but they really liked to smoke hand-rolled cigarettes and drink cheap whisky out of red plastic cups. The cups reminded me of college beer pong. I declined a few times. I came to India for a spiritual experience. I didn't come to get wasted on the dusty streets of Delhi.

I noticed my prudishness was being interpreted as rudeness. All they knew about me was that I was the friend of a relative, and that I was in India for yoga. They tried their best to knock me off my high horse. So, in the spirit of friendliness, I gave in to drinking and smoking with these boys. I laughed when they laughed and did my best to fit in. The whole experience of being surrounded by a clique of rowdy friends reminded me of how guys would gather on stoops on brownstones back home. I was waiting for some lip-smacking to happen, but it was very rare to catch sight of a scantily clad lady on the streets. The boyish camaraderie was all the same minus the lip-smacking. The whisky and cigarettes became a cultural bridge, and for a few moments, I was one of the guys.

In the morning, I hacked up the night's cigarettes and got into a taxi, Rishikesh-bound. Delhi to Rishikesh is less than the distance between New York City and Providence, Rhode Island, but it takes six to eight hours to get there because of the poor road conditions. Cars, trucks, large eighteen-wheelers, auto-rickshaws, cows, oxen, horses, donkeys, bicycles and motorcycles with families of five hanging off the side would all travel on a narrow two-way road. I was a virgin traveler no more. I officially popped my cherry when I decided to get in a car for an eight-hour road trip. Every second, it seemed like we were about to be in a head-on collision with a stubborn cow or truck carrying too much cargo. It was too exhausting to maintain a state of freak-out. I let go of the need to look at my surroundings and constantly know where I was. "Let go, and let God," as I had heard many a time before. I had to chill out and embrace the bumpy ride.

Eight hours later, I arrived at the reception area of Anand Prakash Ashram and was greeted by the boyishly cheerful Pramod-ji, the manager of the ashram. Sitting on the sofa was the guy I came to train with, Yogirishi Vishvaketu (I called him Vishva for short). I wasn't in the best state to be received by anyone, let alone by the yoga guru himself. However, his beaming smile was infectious, and I felt this amazing jolt of vitality reenergize my weary and achy body.

I had missed the morning yoga class and could not wait to attend the afternoon class.

While most people in my program spent some time traveling throughout India, and others arrived the day before the training, I purposefully arrived a month earlier to settle and root. The thought of backpacking was always appealing, but in reality, it drained me. I much preferred discovering the ins and outs of Rishikesh without the pressures of time. I also knew that when the training started, I would not have as much time to leave the ashram.

The daily ashram schedule was rather mild in comparison to many other places that enforced silence all day. We started the day with morning yogic cleanses between 5:30 and 6 AM. This mainly involved using a neti pot to clear the mucus out of the nasal passages, followed by *kappalabhati* purification breathing. This was in preparation for all the deep breathing we would do in yoga class at 6 AM. I particularly enjoyed learning how to do the *sutra neti*, which involved using cotton string that looked like a shoelace. The purpose was to floss the nostrils by threading one end of the lace up the nose, while the other end came out of the throat. It made perfect sense. If we floss our teeth to preserve our gums, why not floss the pollution out of our nasal passage?

Between 6 and 7:45 AM, we had our yoga class with Vishva. His cuing was in simple English without the flurries of anatomical precision. His cues were received and felt through the spaces between his words. His playfulness of spirit mesmerized the room. Vishva's gentle, flowing style of hatha yoga was not as physically vigorous as the ashtanga and vinyasa styles I was exposed to back home, but I always felt purified on a deep level. Often times, he would finish the class with an infectious group laughing session that left us in tears. I always left his classes on a cloud of smiles.

The bell would then ring sharply at 8 AM, calling us to breakfast. We would file into the dining hall dressed in pristine white with the food trays from our rooms. After everyone received a helping of food, we chanted blessings before eating. Vishvaji echoed a teaching that Zen master Thich Nhat Hanh also taught: The purpose for blessing the meal before eating was to raise the vibrations of what we were about to put into our bodies.

By raising our vibrations, we could digest at the most optimal level. Eating in silence without the distractions of chitchat, I was able to immerse in the total experience of eating. I never thought it would be so refreshing to concentrate on thoroughly chewing my food and let go of the pressures of socializing. That silence allowed me to become more aware of how I thought and felt during the act of eating. The regulated stillness allowed me to realize that I was the author of my own experiences. If I found myself stuck in a field of anxious thoughts related to the past or the future, the silence forced me to quickly return to the present moment. I could either choose to eat in the thickness of distressed thoughts or let them go.

There is something indescribable about the energy of being in a spiritual community of like-minded seekers that accelerated me into a higher state of presence than if I were on my own. On an average New York City day, eating was a rushed tossing of food down my throat as I ran from one appointment to the next. It was such a relief to relish in the joy of eating without the pressures of doing anything more than the activity at hand. Simplicity is simply nourishing!

By 8:30 AM, you could hear the ashram pundit chanting the Gayatri mantra while preparing the fire puja in the garden below the dining hall. This mantra is a vital part of an ancient tradition from the Vedic times. It invokes the element of fire in our lives by paying homage to it through daily ritual. From an ashram newbie's perspective, our daily fire ceremony could be quite daunting with all the chanting and gestures of offering. For me, the whole process bore an air of familiarity. Growing up watching my father at the family altar make daily offerings to my ancestors never made more sense to me than it did at the ashram. Ceremony was about cultivating self-respect through paying respect to the fires of creation, and the fires of transformation. It was a daily reminder that the energy which creates the sun and the energy that drives our lives is much greater than our insubstantial, ego-based wants. It was a reminder that we are merely pieces of the grand puzzle and are designed to exist in harmony with the universe.

Vishvaji told us that during one of the most challenging moments in his life, he chanted the Gayatri mantra 300,000 times in solitude, and the universe gave him the answers he needed. He often joked that his insights and revelations were like a computer download. If he didn't immediately know the answer to a question, he would say, "I will let you know tomorrow after download."

The Gayatri mantra played in the background of my dreams most nights sleeping at the ashram. And whenever I chanted it during the fire puja, I instantly felt a deep connection to the sun that shines over the earth as the sun shining within me. It was an experience of the macrocosm merging with the microcosm. Mantra was just another way for me to turn off logical thinking and switch on my capacity to feed my heart and soul.

We held chant books in our hands and followed the pundit and Vishvaji's lead when it came to chanting their selection of the Vedic mantras. The whole ceremony involved offering ghee and wood chips; sometimes, during special occasions, flowers or sweets were used. An urn of water was placed near the *havan*, or firepit, which received the life force energy of all our blessings. After the twenty-five-minute fire puja was finished, Vishvaji would fertilize the garden with the blessed water.

When I was little, I was always enchanted by Christmas hymns and Gregorian chants, and secretly wished my parents would take me to church so I could fit in with the rest of Christian America. Even though my father is a staunch Buddhist, we never went to temple. The family altar prayers were always performed solo, and occasionally he would hold our hands and pray for us, but he never taught us to do it for ourselves. The group chanting during the fire pujas fulfilled what my heart pined for all these years. It felt so right. During my stay there, I effortlessly recited the Vedic mantras to the point where people would ask how long I had studied in order to chant them from memory. Like Vishvaji said, it felt like a massive download that happened by simply arriving into my presence. It was as if my cellular memory bank was being reactivated. I had the strangest dreams that would fade from recollection ten minutes after waking up, but I knew those dreams in Rishikesh offered a profound reconnection to my lifetimes long past.

After the fire puja, if you were not in the teacher training program, you had the option of doing *seva*, or "selfless service." Normally, it comprised cleaning duties in the yoga halls, kitchen prep or administrative help in the reception area. It left plenty of time to stroll into town or to take a peaceful walk along the Ganga River before the 4 PM yoga class. Dinner was more festive than breakfast. At 6 PM, Vishvaji started short call-and-response chants to elevate the mood in the room, followed by our routine food blessings and happy eating. Some evenings, we had *kirtans*, or devotional chanting. I cherished these moments because it wasn't about how well we sang. It was about expressing our desire to connect with our divinity.

Ashram life was modest and simple. We ate simple *sattvic* food, which is a vegetarian yogic diet emphasizing seasonal foods designed to promote maximum life force energy. After waiting tables, running from audition to audition, rehearsing for shows, and living the hectic life of an actor in the hustle of New York City, the structure and routine of being in the ashram was a huge sigh of relief. I finally had time to ground and nurture the parts of myself I had neglected.

After a week of regular yoga, breathing, meditation and chanting, it finally hit me. I somehow blocked out the fact that I had written a letter to my parents and didn't call to see how they were receiving the news of my coming out. All of this talk about authenticity, and here I was in India hiding from the truth. I bought a phone card and braced myself for the most anticipated phone call of my life. My father picked up the phone.

There were many awkward silences before I brought up what he and Mom thought of my letter. There was a sad softness in his voice that was a mixture of concern and disappointment. He played up the concern and pleaded for me to come home so that we could "fix" it together. My mother then grabbed the phone from him. She didn't tiptoe around the subject in the hesitant tone my father adopted. My mother's style was more like mine, uncensored candor bred with verbal diarrhea.

Her barrage of questions came from a place of curiosity. Like an unpolished Sherlock Holmes, she asked things like "Were you molested as a child?" "Who molested you?"

Yes, Mom, because homosexuals are like vampires and are converted through the touch of dirty old men on the prowl, I thought. I lacked the Chinese to express my snide remarks.

"You practicing yoga and being a gay, makes you a hypocrite. It's not natural." "What did I do wrong?" "Do you really hate us that much?"

Another ride on Momma's guilt express. I wondered how supporting my authentic truth with an ancient holistic system was against the natural order. And it was so skillful how she made me feel bad for me being gay while blaming herself all at the same time.

I had expected World War III and an ultimatum to stop my gayness at once or be disowned forever. I did not have the smoothest relationship with my parents growing up, and the wounded child in me still feared being rejected. And when the rejection didn't come, it was a tremendous breakthrough for me. I had always projected expectations based on the worst-case scenario, all of which created excuses and delay tactics. Instead, my parents, in their own bizarre way, expressed concern and worry for me. They treated me more like I had a disease instead of with outright hate and the stripping away of my title as their son. I thought, *This is actually not as bad as I thought. I can handle this level of dysfunction.* As misguided as their questions and statements were about my letter, it was such an improvement on how I thought it would go down.

The phone call ended in hushed to-be-continued voices. I told them that I was not coming home immediately and would return in three months' time like I had originally set out to do. They wished me well and told me to take care, and I wished them the same. In the spaces between the lines, we were subtextually establishing that we all needed time to process how we were going to deal with this. *Phew.* I can't even begin to describe the load that left my shoulders after that moment. I finally tasted my first step toward emotional freedom by confronting the two people who were the source of my suffering.

Everyone I met in Rishikesh was going through something big in their lives. The place seemed to attract soul seekers from all over the world. People came because they were tired of the same old way of being. The collective charge of us all congregating at a place with a unified mission definitely catalyzed a massive internal shift.

The five weeks before my advanced yoga teacher training course were jam-packed with spiritual activities. I enrolled in a course on Ayurveda and Ayurvedic massage with a woman doctor named Dr. Usha Vaishnava. Everything also seemed to fall into place for me to receive a Reiki initiation with Shantih Mai who lived at the Omkarananda ashram across the Laxman Jhula bridge.

Shantih Mai wasn't easily accessible via email or phone, and I was told that I could find her at the German bakery between noon and 1 PM. I felt like I was in an old spy movie, going to the bakery at an assigned time. I instantly gravitated to this older German lady with starry blue eyes. I was already doing energy work by that point and was quite aware of Reiki from previous sessions in New York. Shantih Mai shared her relationship with Reiki and how the three levels of courses would unfold. I was on my here-is-the-courageous-new-me kick, and I decided to go big or go home. I enrolled into all three courses and became a sixth-generation certified Reiki master of the Usui Reiki lineage.

In Reiki, there is no right or wrong. It's an intuitive healing practice where I, the practitioner, focus on using healing symbols through inner visualization and physically drawing them in space to create a connection between the divine and the recipient. I have always been sensitive to energies and remember distinctly as a child willing my body to cool down when it got too hot during the summers on the muggy subway platforms. I would command a chilling electrical current that ran from my belly button up to the base of my skull. The directed current instantly gave me goose bumps and the sensation of being cold, and shortly after, an unbearable hot summer day was tolerable. This early discovery gave me access to an important energy channel for this moment when I started delving more deeply into energy work.

During our Reiki sessions, I found the initiation processes vague and detached from the physical story of what was happening. My mentor Courtney taught me how to blueprint energy patterns through very specific pathways that I could clearly feel and chart through my body and another's body. The movement of energy was always related to the physical and emotional story. A few months earlier, I was doing regular bodywork on a client who had stage four breast cancer. The physical work of cradling and releasing the physical adhesions in her shoulders was directly connected to her emotions of unexpressed sadness. Through touch, I was able to feel the sadness she felt for leaving this life sooner than planned. I didn't tell her at the time, but I felt that the purpose of my bodywork sessions were to help her cross over. She lived for a few more years, and I found out later that she passed during my second visit to India.

Firsthand, I know how powerful energy work is in its ability to help transmute physical and emotional pain, and I was honored to be studying with masters in their field.

However, I found the Usui Reiki work to be more disembodied than I thought it would be. It was very different from what I was used to. Shantih Mai was not interested in reading and interpreting the client's stories as the energy work unfolded. She focused on trusting and allowing universal life force energy to flow through her into the client from a place of neutrality.

If someone shared a revelation that came about from the Reiki session, it would be news to her. To come fully into Reiki mastery meant to empty oneself of ego and become an empty vessel. So, I found it a bit disconcerting that she certified me as a Reiki master when I knew I had quite a way to go in letting go of ego. I took it as a lesson in trust when she left me to find my own way to self-mastery without the confines of a deadline.

My meeting of Swamiji, who was a Reiki grandmaster, added to this great shift that was happening in me. He played the role as my spirit guide in India, even more so than my yoga teacher, Vishva-ji. One day after my Ayurveda massage training was complete, I was looking for a music ashram to learn how to play the harmonium. The sign to Devi's Music Ashram was confusing. It might as well have said, "Go to the temple, walk north, then south, then circle around yourself like a fool and maybe take 200 steps to the right, and you might find us if the gods allow." My getting lost and confused led me to Swami Amitanand's house. Here was this shirtless man with a big pot belly wrapped in an orange *dhoti* from the waist down. I was instantly drawn to him and asked him where Devi's Music Ashram was. He also gave me directions that made no sense. Before I left, I asked him what he did, and he said he taught Reiki, and invited me in for tea. I decided no because I was on a mission, but I took note of the sign above his house—Osho Reiki. I did not find the ashram and would only find it two years later when I returned to India.

A couple of days later, I was compelled to show up at the Osho Reiki man's house and have tea with him. I brought with me a lightning stone from Africa that I had bought in Union Square in New York from some guy peddling gemstones. I was on my way to yoga class, and this black stone in the shape of a spearhead caught my eye. I bargained the price down to forty bucks and brought it to Courtney. She intuitively picked it up and placed the base of the stone at the base of my skull, and we both had massive energy twitches in the form of physical tremors for a good minute. She basically electrocuted me with the stone. It reminded me of the time I wandered into a Peruvian shaman's workshop on campus in Geneseo. I don't remember if it was culture day, or what, but it intrigued me, and I decided to sit through the shaman's show and tell. He spoke through a translator, and explained how he used spearheads, swords, rattles and other shamanic tools for energy work and soul clearing. He used a similarly shaped object that triggered a volunteer into having spasmodic shakes. Courtney told me, "Take this stone with you to India, and someone there will show you what to do with it."

I entered Swami Amitanand's house. He was having tea with a yogi friend of his. I was there with a friend, Katrina, who I met at the ashram. She was also interested in what he had to offer. He did an energy test on us. After the energy test, he exchanged approving looks with his friend, and spoke a few words of encouragement in Hindi. Then he told me he would accept me as his disciple. I felt so special and excited that I passed his little energy test, and I brought out my lightning stone. "By the way, do you know what this is? And what is it for?" He took the stone in his hand, examined it for a few seconds, turned the base of the stone onto the center of my brow, and send a jolt of electricity into my skull. The jolt was a bit more than I was prepared for. I sank to the ground and shook wildly like the time I stupidly stuck a wire hanger into an electrical socket and electrocuted myself when I was ten.

"You should not be playing with such things, my dear," he said. He gave me back my stone, and I wrapped it up, said thank you, and went back to the ashram.

I was at a loss for words and stunned. This man might be the teacher I was in India to find. The universe seemed to guide me to him when I initially was looking for music lessons. More than studying Reiki with him, I was excited to have potentially met my spiritual guru.

Unlike Shantih Mai's group lessons, I had intensive private lessons with him that went on for twenty-one days over the course of a month. His wife sometimes cooked delicious meals for me while I joked with his thirteen-year-old computer whiz son Arpit about him becoming the next CEO of Microsoft when he grew up. It felt like I had left my family in New York to reunite with another family that I belonged to in another lifetime. I felt so comfortable and at home with them.

Swami Amitanand was an Osho sannyasi and lived with Osho in the eighties when he was still alive. During that time, he studied Osho's active meditation techniques and also learned Reiki. It was very different from the traditional symbols that I had learned from Shantih Mai. Instead of using the symbols of the creator of the Reiki method, Dr. Usui, my time with Swamiji was a journey of me becoming my own master, which meant that I needed to create my own symbols and not use someone else's.

When I felt inspired after my self-healing practice, I was assigned to doodle different symbols that came to me. He would tell me which ones were authentic and could be used. Eventually, I created three go-to symbols that I would use constantly in sessions with my clients later on. While Shantih Mai instantly allowed us to work on client bodies, Swamiji restricted me to do Reiki on myself for 180 hours. He said I was not a clean enough channel yet. In other words, I was not clean enough to be helping others. I respected the fact that he was an advocate of responsible and sustainable training. He was not about to let his disciples run amok and negligently Reiki anyone. It was my vetting period, and I needed to put in the time to earn the right to offer Reiki to others.

He warned me of the dangers of practicing Reiki with a swollen ego. He once miraculously helped a paralyzed man walk again. In return, he received many opportunities from wealthy donors to create a center, but he was always wary of accepting money that carried the agenda of exploiting or diluting the purity of Reiki. He shared a story of one of his classmates, who went off to start a successful healing practice in Switzerland working specifically with a wealthy clientele. Her specialty was in eliminating cancers. There was nothing wrong with working with a certain demographic of people, except she became materialistically motivated over time and charged an exorbitant amount for healings. She was able to live an affluent lifestyle and put her children through well-to-do private schools. Many years went by, and she returned to Swamiji with a stomach ulcer that became cancerous very quickly.

"What happened, dear?" Swamiji asked her.

"You were right. Everything that I did came with a high price." The healings she offered had an agenda. She created hooks in the wealthy to keep them coming back to her so that she could fund the lifestyle she wanted. Swamiji called this "Reiki bouncing." Everything backfired. He didn't believe there was anything wrong with her charging 8,000 dollars for working with those who could afford it, but the intention behind her work led to her downfall.

I had a different experience with energetic hooks. However, mine was not in the realm of material motivation; I became attached to the emotional stories of other people. I was attached to feeling needed. Unconsciously, I assumed the role as the savior or the martyr. I was addicted to helping people release pain by taking it on for them. It gave me a sense of power. The winter before, when I started getting more bodywork clients, I literally turned yellow for seven days. I had no strength to leave the house. I would get up, try to eat, vomit, cry in the shower, and go back to sleep. I was taking on the energy of my clients' stories without releasing it properly. My mother came and brewed herbal tonics and potions to bring my fever down. She was always good at being a mother when I was suffering, even though she found moments to scold me for not taking care of myself. Many people perceive attachment to be only of a material nature. I know firsthand that the attachment to power and the need to feel like I belonged created an equally dangerous energetic hook that endangered my health.

The training I went through with Swamiji to decondition these unconscious attachments was intense. In his house, I was blindfolded in his meditation room for one-hour active meditations that involved erratic shaking, sometimes gibberish, shouting, and whirling like a dervish until I got dizzy and banged my head against a wall. Most of the active meditations had some physically unsettling component at the start to break me out of my head in order to connect me. As a result, the last fifteen minutes of the meditations were always emotionally and energetically heightened experiences. I was transported out of time and felt an indescribable bliss. At the same time, my body also went through this unusual process of releasing grief from many years of restrictive behavior patterns. It was like experiencing sadness and joy simultaneously; an orgasm of tears.

The toughest period was when I was instructed to go through four days of total silence, of which I spent the majority of the time sobbing hysterically. It was my time of release. It was just me and myself dealing with my own rawness. I sat in a café listening to all the conversations happening around me one day, and I caught myself opening my mouth to correct someone's answer about something I knew. It wasn't even that important. Why did I feel the need to correct and instigate all the time? I stopped myself just in the nick of time and thought, *I don't need to be right all the time. Just let it be. Why were you just about to start a battle over someone else's simple conversation?*

The experience led me to realize how addicted I was to the fight. My whole life up until this point was a constant battle to be accepted and loved. I realized the more I fought, the more I distanced myself from acceptance and love. I also realized during this sacred time that most of the small talk I did in daily life was artificial and drained me energetically. My assignment on silence was not only a practice of being verbally and mentally quiet, but also a practice of unlearning the extra layers of conditioned crap that stifled the truest version of myself.

I learned many things about myself with Swamiji. And without a doubt, my interactions were all trying to teach me how I relate to myself and thus the world around me. Ultimately, every ancient kernel of wisdom, anecdotal story, chant, yoga class, meditation experience and healing practice was there for the purpose of self-realization. A grand event, it seemed. Self-realization or enlightenment always felt like it would be this monumental occurrence that only happened as an old hermit on the mountaintop. But I now see it as an ever-evolving process of unfolding. Just like the universe will continue expanding until it no longer does, we too will continuously look in the mirror and question our thoughts, decisions and actions until we no longer exist in this form. It is part and parcel of our destiny in this incarnation on this planet. We are here to consciously expose the unconscious. We are here to rewrite our stories of a conditioned way of being. We are here to break beyond our limits and ripen into the vastness that we already are.

CHAPTER 10

THE ASTROLOGY
READING THAT TURNED
INTO SOUL THERAPY

ॐ

*"Be humble for you are made of earth.
Be noble for you are made of stars."*

SERBIAN PROVERB

After my peaceful morning ashram routine, I would head to my Ayurvedic doctor for my three-week *panchakarma* program. Panchakarma was a deep internal cleanse to reset my gut, involving fourteen days of enemas, a minimal yogic diet, Ayurvedic massage therapies and a few other bits here and there. Some people had twenty-one days to do it, but Dr. Usha didn't think I was that internally imbalanced to start. I enjoyed my morning chats with Dr. Usha. She was full of knowledge and in some ways played another counselor role in my imaginary spiritual court. Her tiny office attracted people needing more than just a deep colon cleanse. And it was here that I scored another serendipitous meeting that the universe had in the cards for me.

In Dr. Usha's humble meeting hub of seekers, I crossed paths with the astrologer Sri Ma Amodini Saraswati, who was also coming in for her panchakarma. The stars were in alignment. I had seen a traditional Vedic astrologer the week before and was unmoved by his dry analysis of my life. I wasn't new to palm readings and tarot card readers asserting their urgent messages with that annoying hint of apocalyptic doom. If I wanted that, I could just walk down Greenwich Village, and wait for a frenzied gypsy woman to yank me off the street into her brownstone basement lair for a fearful list of "If you don't do this, you'll be doomed to . . ." Up until that point, I had only experienced psychic counsel through the mode of old-school premonition. Sri Ma Amodini Saraswati's four-hour session was not that; it was the kind of counsel I had been waiting for. It was life-changing. She spoke to my soul and empowered me to relinquish my fear-based ego.

I made an appointment for ten days after our initial meeting. Successfully completing the twenty-minute rickshaw ride to her house was the first step. Directions were never going to be smooth for me in India. I missed my stop and got off by the newspaper distribution building. I backtracked along the rickshaw route to find her apartment complex. Once I was there, it wasn't difficult to figure out which one was hers. Her front door overflowed with green plants and beamed a magnetic vibe. The door was already ajar, and I heard her voice from the adjacent room: "Come in."

Her head of short, mannish hair and eyeglasses reminded me of an eccentric Jeff Goldblum minus all the comedic flair. Sri Ma Amodini was an unorthodox Indian woman living solo in this sizeable apartment by Indian standards. In our chitchat, she mentioned briefly that she had received a PhD in social work at the University of California. Needless to say, I was impressed and inspired by her entire aura. How inspiring it was to meet this unmarried Indian woman who went against the grain to devote her life to helping others find their true path.

At her front door, she had an altar dedicated to Mahavatar Babaji, who I had read about in Paramahansa Yogananda's *An Autobiography of a Yogi*. Babaji is an Indian saint said to have lived for hundreds of years in the Himalayas and who only appears to a select number of disciples in person and in visions. This was her guru, no doubt, and it felt as if Babaji imbued her apartment with so much spirit that I instantly felt it in my bones. With all the previous energy work with my mentor, Courtney, my system was like an antenna for sensing the invisible.

After a few moments of pleasantries and drinking water, Sri Ma Amodini went straight to work. She was like a television set receiving waves of information from the beyond. Instead of feeling on guard, as I did in the past with other readers, I listened in awe and fascination. Other readers or so-called spiritual counselors who gave me readings seemed enshrouded in a sphere of agenda, but Sri Ma did not. She had pre-assessed my Western and Vedic charts and weaved her reading with the messages of the Celtic cross tarot card spread and an Osho Zen tarot spread. It didn't feel prescriptively apocalyptic, and it was so much more than a reading; it was soul counseling.

"Have you connected with the Ganga River yet?" Sri Ma Amodini Saraswati asked. I told her about the week earlier when I went river rafting north of Rishikesh through the "wall."

On the way to the drop-off point while driving along the cliffs of the Himalayan foothills, the rapids looked small and slow-moving from the road above. I was hoping to not repeat my first rafting experience in the South of France where I capsized with my friend Magali and got carved up by sharp rocks when I was twenty.

The first thing they told us when we got off the van was that 50 percent of the rafts capsize on the first pass. The narrow pass framed a robust cluster of waves that seemed to thrash back and forth from wall to wall in an infinity symbol. Our guide instructed us that if we went overboard, we had to swim to the right to ensure not getting mauled by the cliff's wall.

My heart beat anxiously as we approached the monstrous grade-four rapids. Just when I thought we were going to successfully paddle over the crest of an oncoming wave, we were thrown back and flipped sideways from the starboard side of the raft, where I was sitting. I had an issue with swimming in open water and a fear of drowning. I was consumed by fear. There was no way I was going down. I grabbed onto the safety line with so much force that I ripped a layer of skin off my hand. I was in the water, but at least I was still holding onto the raft. Then a fat Indian guy who was double my weight cannonballed into my shoulder and kicked my head into the river.

The Ganga was not going to let me off that easily, it seemed. My vision went as the contact lenses slid out of my eyes. The chilling Himalayan water caught me by total surprise. My conscious mind then remembered, *Swim right like the guide said.* As I swam right, the guy who knocked me in managed to get another solid kick to my head in his hysteric attempt at swimming. *Oh no, I have to move away from him,* I thought, *or I'm going to get a concussion and drown. What am I going to do?* I refused to become another statistic of amateur nonswimmers who idiotically get into the Ganga year after year.

Focus, Johnson, focus! Find that yogic calm. All of a sudden, my mind went blank and an inner guidance instructed me to not only swim right, but down. So I went down. The waves submerged me even while wearing a lifejacket. I swam away from the heavy kicker, away from the raft, away from the surface. I kicked toward the darkness where the sunlight became dark purple. An incredible feeling of surrender took over me. Contrary to my instinct to struggle, I followed the river instead. I swam with her current effortlessly and let her carry me downstream.

My breath and my thoughts paused. I only felt silence and support from something much greater than me. It was like my Lion King moment in my freshman year dorm, but underwater. After what seemed like an hour in a void, an oar was suddenly thrust into my hand and broke the nothingness. The support crew had followed the rafts in kayaks and were sent downstream to collect those of us who went overboard. I was full of unnecessary tension and fear for no reason. The universe had my back, and I just needed to trust.

She chuckled at my story and summarized my introduction to the Ganga.

> The river teaches surrender, because if you are struggling with the current, you will drown. Go with the flow, then you will achieve mastery. The mind will not permit this surrender because the mind wants to control the whole entity. The minute we connect to the big forces of nature, the mind falls silent. It is teaching the mind that there is something bigger in the universe.

She expounded on the importance of me learning to shut up and get out of my own way.

> The mind is a creature of the past. It is always in the past bringing up past failures and past feelings of inadequacy. Sometimes, you just have to say, "Cut the crap. Stop it, I'm the boss." The mind must fall in line.

A few weeks later, I met a numerologist from England who articulated this "cut the crap" business in a way that appealed to my rational mind. I asked him about past life regressions for self-reflection purposes. He counseled against it. He said,

> Wisdom is the understanding that we have two aspects of our intelligence. And that they are completely different. The whole of Freudian psychoanalysis and regressing into past lives is an imposition of the conscious mind upon the unconscious mind because the conscious mind is the masculine part of our intelligence that wants to put everything into boxes. It labels things: this is a computer, and this is a bed. The unconscious mind is the present part of our mind doing everything unconsciously according to its natural program. It doesn't label; everything is one, everything is present. And so, enlightenment is about the conscious mind finally realizing what Jesus, Buddha and Lao Tzu did. Jesus said, "I can of myself do nothing. My father doeth the work. Everything is already being done. The great play is unfolding by itself. All I have to be is utterly present within. The kingdom of heaven is within."

I found it so provocative every time I encountered a spiritual teacher who quoted the Bible in a way that highlighted truth and love above bureaucracy and dogma. I had to study the Old Testament senior year of high school in English literature, and felt how hateful and unfair the Christian God was. I detested the absolutism of the gospel and during literary debates was always on the side of angry science-based atheists. But then there were people like Swami Amitanand, Osho and this numerologist who highlighted how religion is essentially a guide to our mastery within. Everyone I met told me the same thing in different ways: to stop being an enemy to myself. And the key was to practice abiding in the simplicity of *being* rather than *doing*, or, in the words of Swamiji, "Do from non-doing."

The idea of doing from not-doing was so paradoxical that I became frustrated. I tried to understand the concept intellectually, but it was beyond that. Sri Ma Amodini's full-frontal attack on my mind and ego allowed me to experience the concept of doing from non-doing rather than merely think about what it could possibly mean. Like how bees can see ultraviolet radiation and humans can't, I had to put on different lens to experience the world from a new perspective.

She created analogies with my astrological chart—simple stories that were to the point and designed to spark this change of perspective:

> The mind has become a kind of devil. The Saturn and Moon are your father and mother influence. And it was difficult. How they are as people doesn't matter. How they came across to you as a child was a painful experience. And because of that, the mind oppresses you. There is a lot of negation and self-doubt. And Virgo at that level is like a merciless critic. So, naturally, the mind has been programmed towards self-criticism and self-hatred. It is time to let go. This image [the tarot card of the Devil] is inescapable. And it is showing you the power of the mind, where you can't relax. It is a picture of nightmares and misery.

The Devil card is the fifteenth major arcana card in the traditional deck of tarot and is portrayed as a satyr (half man, half goat with the wings of a bat). It symbolically

represents our battle with our personal demons rather than the personification of the Lord of Hell.

Sri Ma had me mesmerized by the message she had for me. I had so many questions, but I patiently listened and absorbed what I could without jumping the gun. I share this excerpt from my recorded session with Sri Ma Amodini because I believe what she was counselling me on was not uniquely my story, but our collective human story:

> You have a rightful place to be where you are on the Earth. Your mission is in partnership with the Divine and the Universe. And you will be helped in that unfoldment. The pre-natal new moon, the new moon before you were born, is a very significant place in the horoscope. And this was on 1 degree Pisces, which is a difficult degree coming into this world. That is why you experienced victimization. It has to deal with your past life experiences with victimhood, which is being highlighted in this life. But everything else shows that you have already achieved karmic balance. That is the assurance you are getting. You are not somebody who has come with loads of bad karma in the background. But there is a hangover in this life from that time. That place is very sensitive and raw inside.
>
> Pisces is the sign of Jesus Christ. So it is a sign that is not exactly martyrdom, but it is about sharing certain values at the forefront. Everyone's wellbeing is important to you. Self-sacrifice doesn't mean putting yourself to the cross. The message of Christ was about resurrection on behalf of humanity. Now, you will be there as a compassionate healer. And in order to do that, you can't suffer like this. With every dying person, you can't suffer the trauma of death. Like that, you can't be a good healer. You will drown yourself. Healers must be detached. Death is not finality. It is not the end. The soul is being released. And who knows what comes? Many souls go on the higher

path. They are happy to be relieved of the pain and the bondage of earthly life. So we need to understand this bigger philosophy, connecting with the truth of existence, beyond the limits of the dualistic mind. Right now, everything is saying that your mind has you in its thrall. Surrender in the river.

All religious practices are designed to keep the mind quiet, whether it is Christian, Islamic, Hindu, or whatever. The mind must not control. Because at that level, the mind is the Devil. If you are here, the mind says you should be there. You are trying to do something special. It will say, "You will fail; why bother?" So the mind is the Devil that keeps us irritated and unhappy. Feeling like a failure. This mind is programmed by other people. Now when I say "my mind," I say it's not mine. It's anything but me. Parents are projecting their own insecurities onto their children. "Don't do that, or you will fail." Those messages make very deep grooves. As children grow up, they are affected by school, friends, society, TV, advertisement, politics, ideology. All this is the stuff of mind control—what other people want out of you. It's not about you. Even you don't know who you are, or what your essence is. So we try to conform and fit in, but we can't. And so the mind becomes like that.

But through the spiritual work, we are connecting to the "I" in meditation. And the soul is the orchestrator in this life. The soul chose this life. The soul chooses everything—which parents to be born to, which society—because this life is very precious and it wants to achieve its goals. Sometimes people suffer horrific abuses, but the soul has chosen to go through that. It's not because of bad karma necessarily. Yes, many people fall by the wayside, but strong souls have come into these situations for a reason. It is like training in the University of Life with the confidence that at the right time, you will come through. And that pain generates healing. The moment there is pain, the flow of healing starts. The pain makes us sensitive. You can only be a healer if you yourself have suffered pain. Just like it is an axiom of power that those who are in power must first have suffered the abuses of power so that they will not do the same. It is the process of becoming sensitive. If you are to heal, you must understand how it feels to be hurt.

So you are on the cusp of major transitions in your life at this point. You are coming to your Destiny. And that is why it is important to heal yourself and to take charge. And that means you need to switch from negative Virgo to positive Virgo. Positive Virgo is happy to be of service. Healing integration. You are a Virgo rising with Chiron on the top. Chiron is an asteroid in the belt between Mars and Jupiter. It is the archetype of the Wounded Healer. And that leads to mastery. Chiron is near the highest point, near the *dharma* point in your horoscope. At the very top. And that means you are meant to be a spiritual healer, educator, communicator, a teacher.

And because of Gemini, the work you will do is intelligent work. To bring about integration. The world is completely fractured. And you are one of the powerful people who will bring about healing and unity. Also Chiron is the rainbow bridge, helping people achieve transcendence from the miseries of the material plane to hope, optimism and transformation. That is why your planets are placed in a particular way.

Life is like a dance of acrobatics. Be in balance even if the ground is shaking. That is the way to live life. So go to the river. I've done underwater meditations for two hours when the river is very forceful. The first time it happened, I was just going for a bath, and then I was guided underwater. A lot of my Tibetan lama practices from my past life connected with me. I was doing *kundalini* work for many years on my own. Six years later, I met my gurus all at the same time. So underwater, I was being taught. I didn't drown. It was training for total equipoise because if the mind is quiet, you are in balance. And if a thought comes and you give weight to the thought, then you get disturbed, then bubbles start to come out of the mouth and nose and you need to come up to the surface for breath. Otherwise, you are at perfect equipoise. And that is total detachment.

The river has many things to offer by way of training. In the river, stay calm. Do the inner work. You will be helped and guided. Once you have let go of all the difficult issues, then pray to be connected with your vision. Especially with the sun. Ask and the answers come. You must be sensitive to receiving the answers. Sometimes, it takes time to filter through our system. I say that I have a brilliant idea, but someone has put it there. Experience this guidance. It is from invisible sources. It is helping us to evolve and detach from the lower forces which want to entrap and enslave us. It is essentially our choice. Do we want to connect with the lower dimensions or the higher dimensions? The higher dimensions bring empowerment while the lower dimensions are bringing loss of control like despondency. It requires faith. You must believe *I'm on the right track. Life is perfect.*

I'm young, and you're very young. You will come into your mastery. So feeling helpless and vulnerable is okay. You don't have enough experience yet. And you are going through deep internal work. Even this *panchakarma* [the Ayurvedic detox] is working at the cellular level, and the Ganga will make light of this. And be happy when you are doing it. With faith and hope, everything will fall into place. Also, practice asking a question of the sun. The river communicates, the sun replies. This is very powerful.

Sun is inspiration, fire. The river is balancing the fire by tempering the body. Ask a question and see how the answer comes. Validate the process. Then wherever you go or not, you are connected with totality. You are never alone. Then in an emergency, if you ask for help, help *must* come. Prayer is a two-way communication. If you pray for something, then the answer comes. Like Christ says, "Ask and you shall receive, seek and you shall find." You are not a child. You are not the person who suffered unknown terrors or betrayals in the past. Now, you are strong. You came to India alone, and you are going through these empowering experiences, meeting so many new people. You are okay. Whatever betrayal you have suffered in the past has been when you were powerless and vulnerable. It doesn't mean you will always be like that. You have to say, "I'm strong. I'm perfect. I'm powerful." Take power over your own life.

She went on and on like this for four hours, feeding me food for my soul. I recorded her so I would be able to review anything I missed during the session, which I didn't do until years later during this moment of writing. Everything she told me in the moment, regardless of whether I processed it logically or not, was all I needed to get off my analytical butt and start taking heartfelt action to change my life. That was the point: Stop thinking and start making profound cellular shifts.

I didn't make it to the river the following day. But the day after, I found a quiet spot that was a ten-minute walk down the mini waterfall near Ramana's orphanage. Normally, the beach there was full of yogis sunbathing or weekenders from Delhi drinking and hollering. But that day it was quiet. Mother Ganga was waiting for me. On approaching the bank of the river, my body shuddered as it recalled the frigidness of the Himalayan water. I stood for a few moments and watched the current relentlessly rush downstream. My ego instantly populated a list of reasons to not do this insane assignment: *The river is polluted and dirty. Look at the litter. Someone caught the Giardia parasite last week going in. It's too cold. The current is very strong...* Like the parent of a child throwing a tantrum, I allowed ego to say what it had to say and waited for its voice to fade.

In Haridwar, the holy city twenty kilometers away, pilgrims bathed in the Ganga daily. I'd seen men entering the river only in their undergarments. Winter was around the corner, so I decided to stay clothed as a compromise with my ego's grumbling over how piercing the water would be. I eventually found a spot where I could solidly plant my feet into the sand, neck deep in water. I felt it was important to submerge my whole body to get me to completely stop thinking. As soon as I went under, the penetrating cold of the water froze my thoughts.

Prayer is a two-way street, right? And I'm supposed to pray without overthinking? I sent the prayer through my body. I used my body to ask with arms outstretched in a gesture of receiving. I asked through my felt sense, instead of using words, to deeply connect to the true me, and to let go of anything that was not authentically me. I stood there in silence emanating this desperate desire to understand who I really was supposed to be. A few minutes passed. Nothing was happening. I continued with patience and faith. Then I started whispering the Gayatri mantra like I was talking to the river and waiting for the sun to answer, like Sri Ma Amodini told me to do. After a few moments, the flood gates opened.

I felt this electric shock of energy surge from the base of my spine into my shoulders. Out of my body was unleashed the ugliest cry I had ever had. A snotty cry where I hiccupped mucus like I was having an asthma attack. I wasn't thinking about anything sad, but my body expressed an unvoiced story. All these years, I told myself intellectually that I was no longer the victim of my childhood. My mind got it, but my body didn't get the memo. The body is the recorder for physical sensations and emotional stories, and I ignored the fact that it needed to acknowledge feeling traumatized. My muscles, bones and tissue also needed to experience this confession to move on once and for all. It was a surreal experience. I felt intense grief, sorrow, anger and rage shoot through me in the fullest way. These were not the easiest of emotions to allow uninhibited expression. Similar to playing a character onstage, but even more surreal because I was playing me. It was as if my higher self had restrained my ego temporarily from interfering so that I could watch it all unfold. I had finally become the conscious observer. All this yoga and meditation wasn't about suppressing my feelings and concealing it. It was about diving into the full sensory experience with total surrender and without attachment to the drama.

From a bird's eye view, I was in sopping wet clothes, neck deep in Ganga water with arms outstretched in a static position of deep yearning. I went inward, and the envisioning process began, like moving through a waking dream. My eyes were closed, and my higher self was perched in the seats of a stadium looking down at the coliseum where all the painful stories played out. I watched the pain of my childhood twitch out of my body in a rhythmic release. I watched as I systematically let go of the stories that kept me limited and small-minded. I let go of all the guilt I felt for being gay and the hate for being born into my family. I let go of all the pressures of expectations: of what my parents wanted of me, what my bosses and teachers wanted of me, and the expectations I had for my friends and lovers. I let go of the pressures of needing to feel special or like I belonged. I dropped the label of actor and performer. Piece by piece, I envisioned my entire body free of all the attachments to the self I had constructed. I was not an actor. I was not a yoga teacher. I was not a Pilates teacher. I was not a bodyworker. I was not a son. I was not a brother. I was not anyone's lover. I was nobody. When the process of release was complete, I felt warm. Incredibly warm and connected with the cosmic flow of the universe. I felt the Ganga cleanse my body of the heaviness that prevented me from fully living the life I was born to live. I felt so light. I was the frequency of light itself. I was an empty shell housing the purity of my soul. I wasn't all these things that I thought I was, or what society had me believing that I was. I was empty.

I stepped out of the river and sat on the sand with my baggy, wet ashram clothes, smiling into the sky. My cathartic release could not have come at a better time in my life. My soul had pre-selected these hardships for me so that I could learn the lessons I needed to learn. Through my ups and downs, I played my part perfectly. From that moment, with newfound awareness and a transition to seeing and feeling with a new lens, I devoted myself to being in flow with the fullness of the universe, not against it. I understood that any project I attempt could end abruptly. That I was in control, but also not in control. My actions would only bear fruit if I remained unattached to the end results. It was the beginning of a new chapter of my life where I set goals without expectations. Marked points without connecting the dots. It didn't mean that I sat back and let the world push me around. It meant that I was a coauthor with life, and had to adapt to the unforeseeable currents. It meant that I had to do from non-doing.

CHAPTER 11

NEW YORK, NEW YORK: WHERE DREAMS ARE MADE TO CHANGE

ॐ

"Being Spiritual has nothing to do with what you believe and everything to do with your state of consciousness."

ECKHART TOLLE

A few months before I left for India, I had an extremely jarring experience with *ayahuasca* which shattered everything about who I thought I was. I had not heard of it before a yoga friend of mine invited me to her secret circle. *Ayahuasca* is known as the vine of death and is traditionally used in the Amazon as spiritual medicine. It's specially brewed by a shaman and used in ceremony to communicate with spirit. And when I took it, I literally felt like I was dying.

I had done some hallucinogens before in a recreational context, but nothing prepared me for my first encounter with the sacred grandmother medicine. A participant kindly offered their house to host the ceremony on Long Island in the quiet backwoods. Little did I know that in Long Island I would be taken somewhere I could never un-see.

I arrived at the beginning of the ceremony, late, with Courtney and another friend, T'ai. We were invited one by one around the circle to share an intention to elevate our individual experiences. As the second person who spoke, I said something vague along the lines of, "I'm here to figure out my life purpose." At the time, I was negotiating between the call of being of service spiritually and my desire to be an actor. The man next to me shared that he was there to make peace with his stage four cancer. There was a recovering heroin addict, a rape survivor, victims of domestic violence, and others. It seemed the majority of the group sought to rise above the darkness.

I felt a little silly for voicing my intention under the banner of life purpose because there were so many other, more painful things to choose from. We approached the shaman one by one and drank the brew with him. Then, a very pregnant silence pervaded the room in anticipation of what was about to happen.

Within thirty minutes of taking the *ayahuasca*, the room started to spin in a nauseatingly frantic way. It felt like I was being forced down the rabbit hole, and the part of myself that is always under control was not happy about it. It knew that once I went down the hole, I would never return the same.

The shaman rattled and sung his *icaros*, or "medicine songs," in Spanish. I started to see the vibrations coming from his mouth and how they traveled around the room. I saw the Virgin Mary and the goddess Kali hovering over my neighbor who was dying of cancer. They were holding him in blessings. Dark entities flew around the room from those who were screaming in pain. Every time someone vomited, I saw the demonic shape that came out of them. I closed my eyes to make it go away, but the visions didn't stop. It was a live Technicolor display of the invisible realms coming at me, in me and through me. The air carried information in the form of sacred geometric symbols, and I was at Mother Ayahuasca's mercy.

My foot became my head and my organs were not contained in my body anymore. I lost all sense of physical reality. In addition to seeing sound waves coming from the shaman's mouth, I could hear the light from the moonbeams entering the room. The rules of physics no longer seemed to apply. Consequently, my mortified rational self, a.k.a. my ego, was writhing in pain. Every time I vomited into the bucket to purge, it felt like I was dying. The whole process was very painful and felt very real. In retrospect, the aspect of me that was fighting to hold onto some semblance of the familiar made it even more insufferable.

I don't know when it was that I finally gave in and surrendered to the mighty forces of the universe and all that it was trying to show me. I know I gave a hell of a fight, and in the end was swept away by forces much larger than my idea of who I thought I was. It was a six-hour trip to the unknown, and when I awoke in the morning, I was in a daze and felt completely shattered. My friends and I gathered our sleeping bags and quietly tiptoed out of the room before everyone woke up for the sharing circle. At 6:45 in the morning, we found a twenty-four-hour diner on the way back to Manhattan. We ate our pancakes in a sullen lull that could have been mistaken for the recovery from late-night partying.

I had been deconstructed from the inside out, and my world was flipped upside down. After days and days of processing this life-altering event, I came to the realization that I could not choose to un-see what I saw. Everything that I had intuitively known and felt kinesthetically through my body from the energetic worlds was made known on a scale that was no longer deniable. The result of my asking the *ayahuasca* to show me my life purpose was loud and clear. And the message was that life would be unspeakably challenging and painful if I ignored my destiny.

During the next few weeks, I made the conscious choice to drop my pursuit of life as an actor and commit to the healing arts. By my entering the darkest chasms of existence, the universe had instilled an unwavering gift of trust in my heart. If I just paid closer attention to the signs that appeared so blatantly in my life, I could not go wrong.

That was just the tip of the iceberg, and it was in India that I began a deeper exploration of what it felt like to fully surrender. The *ayahuasca* pushed me out of the shadows into claiming and living my truth more. Like my ex inspiring me to come out to my parents, the *ayahuasca* was a big kick in the butt.

Upon my return to New York, I had answered a lot of questions, and knew I had returned home forever changed. My virgin trip to India was full of magical moments of meeting like-minded souls searching for something greater than themselves. I treasured my time there and already missed the ashram routine. There was a joyful timelessness to how the days passed in India. But I knew I had to let it go. I could not help but feel a bit down on myself, similar to how I felt post-ayahuasca. I wondered if I could really be successful in applying all these spiritual realizations in the concrete jungle of New York. What if I couldn't do it?

Before landing, I envisioned being comforted by the fact that my homecoming would be experienced from a new pair of eyes. I was gone three months, but it felt like three years. I could hear my spiritual teachers reminding me, "We are already enlightened, and we only forgot." I now knew that I was designed to carry out my destiny of service and play my part in humanity's awakening. The thought of it was still more scary than exciting. For the first time in my life, I couldn't see a clear path into the immediate future. I knew things could not continue the way they had been. And I was completely uncertain of what was next for me.

I didn't know how my parents would coexist or not coexist with their now-out gay son, and I for sure didn't know if I was going to follow through completely on leaving acting behind. Did it mean stopping auditioning completely? Did it mean I only auditioned for commercials and projects that required less time-commitment? Or did it mean stopping it altogether? I had to negotiate the terms with myself.

My concerned parents were waiting for me on the other side, looking to fix me at every turn. I tried to detach from the conversations where they suggested acupuncture, herbs and psychotherapy to try and rehabilitate me from gay to straight. I was unsuccessful at keeping my cool. I became enraged and lashed out. What happened to all that meditation and that state of peace I experienced on the banks of the Ganga? It seemed like I was back at square one.

I found myself still auditioning for small projects, and even doing a few projects. I was unable to fully leave the world of the actor behind. My ego thrived on the ambition filling the air everyone breathes in New York. I was caught in the same loop again. Split. Spread thin. Trying to actualize multiple projects and multiple desires in a way that left me feeling depleted and repeating the same mistakes again.

For the remainder of 2012, life seemed to speed me away from the experience of releasing layers and layers of illusion into the Ganga in India. How was it that managing Studio Anya, a holistic center for wellness, was becoming stressful? It was almost impossible to apply all the self-care techniques and live in the ever-present Zen that I was able to access during my three-month soul search in India. Was it me? Was it New York? Or both?

I felt like I was suffocating. And when the opportunity came from my yoga teacher Vishva to teach at Anand Prakash Ashram for six months, I was torn. My soul screamed at the chance to return to India. My ego thought, *Why would I volunteer for six months teaching for nothing, when I am finally making a sustainable living doing it already? What else do I have to learn?*

My decision to return to India was made easier when my mother moved into the guest room of the house that my sister and myself had newly purchased together. She was fighting again with my father about something trivial. After high school, the way they fought shifted massively. It was more passive aggressive and less explosively violent. And my mother never voiced what was bothering her. Instead she would emotionally take it out on the world by claiming she had been wronged by life and that nobody truly cared about her. She was an angry victim who secretly wanted a soft caress but would attack like a feral cat if we got too close.

I had no idea why she was angry at my father this time, but I really didn't care because it was the same petulant behavior that I had seen time and time again. When my mother became this way, she looked for a project to occupy her time. And what better project than to help out her unmarried son and unmarried daughter who were living a busy New York City life? My brother was living with his then-girlfriend and now-wife. He was fortunate to not have to bear with the overwhelming smothering that my mother is capable of.

My mother's sole aim in life was to raise grandchildren and to bask in the glory of her successful American-born children. Her abrupt move into our house was her way of trying to actualize her intentions. After not living with her since I was eighteen, to see her night and day as a grown-up twenty-seven-year-old was jarring. The pluses of having her around were that she would cook and clean for my sister and me. The minuses outweighed any amount of gourmet home cooking or laundry that she could have done for us.

My parents love calendars. They are obsessed with when things are due and how much time they have before the next Chinese holiday. I suppose they give meaning to their mortality by tracking their achievements through marked events. One day, I came home to a living room decorated with not one, but four calendars. My mother was gifted with a calendar of smiling naked babies in diapers and was inspired to get three others that echoed the same motif. In secret, she told my sister it was a psychological approach to help me out. The hope was that the images of smiling babies eating their toes would subversively straighten out my crossed wires. As if I would miraculously fall in line with my many baby-popping relatives who blindly complied with the progeny imperative.

After not having the chance to settle in my new house, the very crux of me was under attack. It was excessive and incessant. Everything my mother does in life is colored by the agony of having to claw away from terrible things. And in successfully doing so, she installed unshakeable belief systems that kept her emotionally safe. There was no point in fighting her. She'll continue to cling to her beliefs like a mother bear fiercely protecting her cub. I most definitely picked up this quality of desperately latching onto the past from her.

What was happening with my mother was mirrored by my role as studio manager at Studio Anya. I was at a place where I knew deep down that I could not stay, as much as it pained me to leave. I felt as if I were a butterfly ripe to emerge from the chrysalis but was stubbornly holding on to the protective sac. I did not want to appear ungrateful to my teacher and mentor, Courtney, for everything that she had given me. We share a bond which spans beyond this lifetime. And the three and half years of training and studying with her was crucial in my development as a practitioner. We even had a brainstorm meeting of building a twenty-year vision together, but no matter how much I tried to suppress the voice, something deep within told me, "No, you need to fly solo right now."

It was a difficult decision to make. At Studio Anya, I was surrounded by a tribe of people who understood me. We spoke the same language. They offered wise counsel when I needed it. Why did I now need to leave the nest and fly off on my own? For several months before my departure, I was overcome with bittersweet sensations of sadness and excitement. I did not want to leave my adopted family of yogis, teachers and healers. I was worried they would feel like I betrayed them if I left. Yet I was also eager at the prospect of taking care of only myself. During those days, I was responsible for a staff of teachers, interns, and various masterful practitioners who were renting our space. The livelihood of Studio Anya was a large part my responsibility, and though it was a great honor, it also did not allow me the time to focus on myself.

My mother's sudden move was the catalyst for a massive shift. The last bits of attachments were crumbling down—everything from my romantic idealizations of a relationship to my fear of being alone. Her daily anti-gay sentiments were unbearable. She kept badgering me about the sanctity of marriage between a man and a woman. My parents' agenda of me marrying a nice Chinese girl and fathering grandchildren was nothing more than the manifestation of their fear of death. I once asked, "What if my brother, sister and I decided to never have children?" "Then what would it all have been for?" my parents replied with an anxious dread.

Before marriage equality was legalized, my parents had corrupted any hope of marriage for me. They were so miserable together, and fought incessantly. Instead of affection, they were verbally aggressive, and I always felt so unsafe when they would erupt into a violent physical throw down. I also hated the thought of conforming to the homogenization of what marriage stood for.

This was the turning point. I had to choose between the familiarity of the daily struggle or throwing myself into the complete unknown. *Am I brave enough to walk away from it all? What if I really do end up alone after all is said and done?* I'd had enough. I had to take action. So what if I was traveling to escape again? I didn't have the time to analyze what was what. At that point, I didn't care. I bought my one-way ticket to New Delhi and knew that it was what needed to happen.

My sister and I had just acquired a new mortgage that wasn't even six months old, and I hopped on a plane back to India. She wasn't exactly thrilled with my decision with all the responsibility of the house falling into her hands. I left my stable salaried job as the studio manager and teacher at Studio Anya—my dream job that was in complete alignment with everything I was becoming. I left behind clients, who I enjoyed teaching greatly, and a group of supportive friends and teachers in pursuit of my emancipation from a stagnant and stifled life. Somewhere deep down, I knew that if I left, the chances of me returning to New York were highly unlikely. I had no clue what was beyond six months of being in India again.

It was another scary thought. Unlike people who have an unquestionable certainty that they will get married and have kids, I had no trajectory. If you are child-bound, for eighteen years your future is selflessly tied to another's. In a way, it is easier to gain a purpose through being a caretaker than to carve a true purpose out of a greater need beyond the family unit. Since my return from my first trip to India, I anticipated a period of building myself into something new, but instead, it was a period of erecting a scaffold and a *Closed for Renovation* sign. My ultimate decision to go was not understood by everyone, but the cost of staying would have been too high.

In dream work, houses and buildings more or less represent our self and our connection to spirit. I practiced meditations where I cleaned out the basement of my house, but I never thought I would completely bulldoze it and rebuild it into something wildly different. I no longer wanted to continue comparing myself to my friends who became successful in the entertainment industry. Being in New York kept me clinging to past notions of who I thought I was supposed to be.

The fear of leaving for six months or more was real. I had been brought up to believe that New York City was the center of the world, and if I couldn't make it there, I would be a failure. *What if people forget who I am? What will I do for money abroad if I run out of savings?* The thoughts swirled and swirled. My devil mind was back in full force. But something in me prevailed. I had been prepared for this challenge. I was reminded of what my spiritual teachers taught me. I was brought back to the lessons of the river. I had to make yet another plunge into the ever-flowing waters of change and learn to accept that wherever I landed in the unknown would be exactly fine. The universe had my back, and every experience, whether positive or negative, would contribute to my spiritual evolution.

CHAPTER 12

INDIA 2.0:
RELEARNING
THE ESSENCE OF
SPIRITUALITY

ॐ

"Spirituality does not mean any particular practice.
It is a certain way of being."

SADHGURU

I had never held a "proper" job, but leaving everything that I knew and a very stable job for an open-ended adventure was more like what someone would do after a successful corporate career. I was compelled to experience my "midlife crisis" at twenty-seven. The mentality I had before I came out to my parents, the waiting-for-the-right-moment mentality, went completely out the window. I didn't want to wait anymore. I wanted to live an exciting life full of adventure and spiritual experiences *NOW*. I didn't care how upset my parents were at my decisions. They called me disrespectful and dishonorable. In the end, they still had to let me go, just as I had to let them and their criticisms of me go. I was the very willful product of my hardcore parents. And the only person who could stop me was me.

Landing in India a second time was a very different experience. In the fifteen months that I had left her, she had gotten more frantic. India didn't feel the same. I didn't feel the same. In the eighty-billion-dollar-a-year industry that is yoga, new ashrams, yoga schools and holistic hotels were spreading like wildfire. The once-more-sparsely populated area of Tapovan in Rishikesh was attracting newer establishments in the name of spirituality.

I thought I had made my peace already with the debate over profiting from those who were confused and lost. Meeting many spiritual practitioners and hearing everyone's philosophy on charging money for a spiritual service kept my opinion about it in flux. Though a price cannot be put on the invaluable benefits of physical, mental, emotional and spiritual wellbeing, it really is a waste of time to judge the philosophies of payment. I know healers in urban cities who charge premium packages for a white-collar demographic, and I know healers who live in the jungle who offer healings for a considerably small monetary exchange. At the end of the day, if the energy exchange between the practitioner and recipient is mutually accepted, it should be of no consequence to anyone else.

However, on my second visit to India, I was still under the impression that the more spiritual sanctums of India would maintain a different integrity, as if spirituality in India would not be susceptible to the lure of financial success.

Swamiji very simply said that the East was trying to emulate the West while the West was doing the opposite. Most of the ashram attendees were Westerners from Europe or the Americas. The majority of seekers in the ashrams were from cultures that believed a successful life equated to a certain kind of career, house, family, and financial status, while it seemed that most Indians were interested in attaining financial success and moving away from their cultural traditions of searching for the eternal truth and the principles of karma and dharma. Even Swamiji's son was more interested in computer science and the global markets than meditation. I asked why he didn't make his son meditate with him, and he replied, "If I force him, what would be the point? I have to respect and honor his desires."

My honeymoon period with India was definitely coming to an end, and my memory of the spiritual homeland was rudely disrupted. I spent a few days with my yoga teacher, Vishva, before he made his departure to Canada. He spent half the year teaching teachers in India, and the other half of the year in Canada and abroad. Now, I was alone, filling his shoes. Before my arrival, I thought that something would naturally click in place when I returned to the ashram, like a new puzzle piece would suddenly appear and make life clearer. It didn't. It was going to be another six months of unpredictable self-discovery.

I felt inadequate stepping into the role as the ashram's yoga teacher. It meant that I was supposed to be a spiritual role model. How was I supposed to be that? I was still figuring things out and was so self-conscious about what my students thought of me. The ashram could house up to forty people. Most of the attendees were flying in from around the world to learn from the cheerful and always laughing Indian yoga master Vishva. Instead, they showed up for a 6 AM class with a twenty-eight-year-old Asian guy who spoke American English. I saw it in their faces: "I flew halfway around the world to study with the Indian yoga master from the website. Who is this guy?"

The typical conversation I had with those coming into the ashram was a probing of my credentials, similar to a cocktail party back home when someone stealthily tries to figure out your material "worth" during the first five minutes of conversation. "What do you do?" "Where did you go to school?" "What part of town do you live in?" The ashram versions of these questions similarly targeted my worth from a spiritual training perspective. "How long have you practiced?" As if spiritual progress could be quantified by years. "When did you graduate your yoga teacher training program?" "Were you always so spiritual?" "You look so young." At twenty-eight, most people you encounter who can afford to travel are bound to be older than you. It was ageism plain and simple. I felt the subtext fueling these questions: What gave me the right to sit on top of the ashram podium and teach to such an international crowd?

I was very defensive at the start, but after a certain number of conversations like that, I learned to answer without my defensive air. It was after a few students of mine who were old enough to be my parents praised me for the work I was doing that I realized I couldn't win everyone over. I had to learn to let go of the people who couldn't move past their idea of an authentic experience. These probers are what I call "guru-hoppers." They hop from guru to guru looking to validate what they already know. And yes, sometimes it is a simple matter of resonating with someone's personality. I had to learn that not everyone was going to relate to how I presented the body of yogic wisdom through my modern lens. Some people needed the stark contrast of learning from someone who was raised in the foothills of the Himalayas from the age of eight versus a feisty New Yorker like me.

The vibe without Vishva was palpably different. The air of reverence for the rules of the ashram was definitely dialed down. Not everyone was there to explore their deep spiritual nature. Some people were in the ashram out of curiosity—another check mark on the bucket list. Some mornings, after yoga class, I was agitated by those who chatted over breakfast when sacred silence in the morning was a known fact. The rules of the ashram created a structure for contemplation and reflection and were to be honored and obeyed. Why were these people willfully disrupting the peace?

I was frustrated at the conscious or unconscious lack of respect from some of the students. Why was it eating at me so much? Was it because I was trying to maintain the peace? Or was my ego bruised by this outright disregard of my authority as the ashram leader? I didn't like it one bit. I felt I shouldn't have to pull the chitchatters aside like some school teacher reprimanding a bunch of ten-year-olds. I secretly wanted the other students to enforce the communal silence. What I wanted didn't happen. So, naturally, my frustration at the noisy rule-breakers extended to the entire student community.

I came to breakfast in anticipation of who would start disturbing the quiet, following that up with piercing looks of disapproval. This happened for two weeks until I finally realized my strict conformity to the rules was encroaching on my peace. If this kind of thing happened in Vishva-ji's presence, it would not faze him. He would forgive and let go. The smile on his face would diffuse any remnants of frustration. How did he do that?

So, one morning, instead of glaring my disapproval, I closed my eyes and imagined that I was one of my noisy interlopers. I imagined where they came from, and what obstacles they had to overcome in order to land them here at the ashram. I stepped into their shoes for a moment and realized that complete silence was too much for them at this stage in their spiritual journey, and their chitchatting was a defense mechanism. Compassion was my conclusion, and I had to respect their process.

That changed everything. Instead of laying all these expectations on people with very different processes and becoming frustrated that they were not telepathically taking my hints of dissatisfaction, I had more open talks with those who were disobeying the ashram rules. It was foolish of me to think they could guess what I was thinking or feeling, and it was not their job to get the rules 100 percent right off the bat. It was actually my job to guide. So, instead of feeling lousy in the morning and hallucinating that everyone was purposefully stepping on my toes, I took the first step in initiating open dialogue.

It was the same thing I experienced the three and a half years I was at Studio Anya as the manager. I was in charge of keeping the harmonious order of the space. I was supposed to supervise the peace while the business grew, which involved making bold decisions. Courtney had given me her trust to make things run smoothly in support of her vision, so I didn't feel I had to communicate my sense of things to the others. I thought communicating what was in my head was a waste of time when I could be using that time explaining things and taking action. I thought everyone under me should just follow orders with no questions asked. As a result, some of my relationships with the other teachers and practitioners became unnecessarily tense. It was the same pattern of being quietly frustrated and avoiding any kind of confrontation for the sake of keeping the peace. And here I was in India repeating this pattern.

It was all *maya*, or what ancient Vedic non-dualist scriptures call an illusion. In Hinduism and Buddhism, maya is that which is unreal. Many spiritual teachers refer to the world in which we live as maya—the technology, the financial institutions, and the ostentatiousness of modern living. I have come to realize that my illusions are composed of the preconceived notions and unconscious patterns from societal conditioning which color what I perceive as real or unreal.

My belief in keeping the peace came from avoidance patterns stemming from years of dodging the charged topic of my homosexuality with my parents. And this same program of avoidance was playing out in my relationship with managing others, disguised as keeping the peace. I was protecting myself from the fear of the projected outcome. *What if they reject me? What if I am misunderstood and will never be understood? What if they lose respect for me?*

The irony was that, through avoidance, I was constantly misunderstood and actually losing respect from others and myself. I had to learn the art of negotiation and relating to others more transparently. Being in the ashram for six months with an international host of students, for most of whom English was not their first language, became a training ground for me to let others into my carefully guarded mind, heart and soul.

During this time in India, I spent a lot more time with Swamiji meditating and absorbing the kernels of wisdom every time he spoke. And though he was very spiritual, he was also very practical and real. There was no false new-age air about him. Spirituality to him was as real as the motorbike he drove. He was a no-bullshit kind of guy, yet he maintained a level of tactful sensitivity before letting me in on the answers.

Swamiji was the kind of guy who preferred to live in flow with the universe. He had very poor advertising, and said that only true seekers would find him, like the day I serendipitously landed on his doorstep by "mistake." Another reason I came back was because, months earlier, Swamiji said he was going to come out of the shadows and build a school for Reiki and meditation, and that he wanted me to be the vice president of the foundation. I was so excited to hear that. Maybe this was my higher purpose, my true calling.

I saw a completely different side of him when we drove up to the land that he was acquiring for his new Reiki school. To get to the land, it was forty minutes north. When I rode on the back of his motorbike for the first time, I was bewildered by his wild driving. I thought we would have a Zen ride up through the mountain roads, but instead he made daring maneuvers and honked more than the normal Indian would. At times, his road rage would come out. He yelled at other vehicles and pedestrians who did not have the right-of-way, shouting in Hindi. I asked him why he was getting so angry at the people.

"I am not angry, dear." What I was mistaking for anger was him passionately playing the part of the ferocious Indian driver. "How can we drive calmly? This is India, my dear."

There was a spiritual lesson he was trying to teach me: When in India, drive as they do. If I imposed my idea of safety or peace on the roads of India, I would perish. In the same way, if I were to impose my idea of anything I thought I knew instead of acknowledging each experience as it truly is in the moment, my spiritual evolution would be dead in the water. My surprise and slight indignation at his driving skills proved that part of me was not fully surrendering to the moment.

I began to accept India more and more as a chaotic blend of things that didn't quite seem to mix, yet worked well in India. India was a land of spiritual gurus oozing sacred knowledge about honoring the divine, while the land suffered from mind-boggling overpopulation, sanitation issues and pollution. On one hand, we witnessed the pristine beauty of a Krishna temple and the devotees within singing and dancing, and on the other hand, we had emaciated and disabled panhandlers begging on the streets and living in filthy squalor. There was so much that didn't add up from a rational point of view.

But maybe all of these contradictions are not meant to be added up. Life is meant to be experienced. The whole range of human emotions is meant to be felt. And all we can do to play our part as the perfectly imperfect piece in the grand puzzle is acknowledge beauty and despair from a place of non-judgment. I can't remember who explained it to me, or if this realization is synthesized from my understanding of all my spiritual teachers. The entire point of the soul reincarnating on the earth is to live the entire spectrum of the human experience, which includes moments of pure ecstasy and moments of insufferable adversity.

I often found myself questioning how I should feel when I passed someone who I perceived to be suffering, like a beggar. *If I offer some change, is this temporary act of kindness to satiate my ego? Give myself a pat on the back for doing something "good"? Which actually is not pure kindness because it's laced with an agenda of trying to feel better about myself rather than truly caring about the beggar? Am I doing it out of pity? Do they even need my pity? Are they going to suffer if I don't help them out with some change? What about all the other beggars on the street? Do I help all of them? If I give to one, should I give to all the others? If I give today, should I give every day? If I don't give every day, then would I be a hypocrite? Or do I ignore them, like they don't exist? Is this part of their soul's karma? Maybe they are spending this lifetime learning humility and their soul elected to return as a beggar.*

So many questions I would ask myself. Then I would reminisce about the mythological stories of Greek gods and goddesses disguised as beggars to test men. Like the story of Zeus and Hermes camouflaging themselves as lowly peasants and asking the people of Tyana to take them in for the night. Zeus and Hermes were turned away by all those who had the material means to take them in but in the end were taken in by the poorest couple, who did not have much. The humble couple, Baucis and Philemon, generously offered to let them stay in their homely cottage. Zeus and Hermes rewarded the couple and destroyed the town of Tyana for their lack of kindness.

It seemed that many travelers with a Western lens on poverty witnessed scenes of begging on the streets with pity like I did. "Oh, I feel bad for them. I feel so sorry for them. Poor them." I realized that these were empathetic remarks generated out of comparing one situation to another. "I come from a life where I have a roof over my head, and eat with a knife and fork, and you don't. So I feel sad for you because you don't have what I have." This was essentially what was being said. Pity acted as a separator; it created a divide between us and them through comparison and by labeling one way as superior and another way as inferior.

Compassion, on the other hand, takes it a step farther: "I see you. I feel you. I can step into your shoes and understand your perspective." Compassion bridges the gap between what is seemingly different and embraces the common ground.

Was it even in my capacity and soul's blueprint to help the beggars on the street? No. That was the authentic answer at the time, which may change in the future. But, in the moment, it was not in my capacity as someone who took all my savings to travel in India and volunteer at an ashram where I wasn't paid a salary. Also, it honestly did not speak to me in the way that the strong desire to understand the purpose of my existence called to me. Just as my call could not be compared to the call that some have to clean up the oceans or take a stand for human rights.

How helpful was it to feel bad for other people in challenging life situations, anyway? If I stepped into a beggar's shoes, life was simpler and wasn't clouded by the dramas of comfortable modern living. In that regard, wouldn't life be easier? Most of my friends and peers were not facing issues of fending for survival. We were more or less trying to figure out our belief systems and how we fit into the world. We were working on our relationship with ourselves and the world. On Maslow's hierarchy of needs, we were somewhere in the middle of the pyramid, while the beggar was still dealing with physical issues of food and safety. I surmised that in the evolutionary scheme of things, every soul is exactly where it needs to be in its journey.

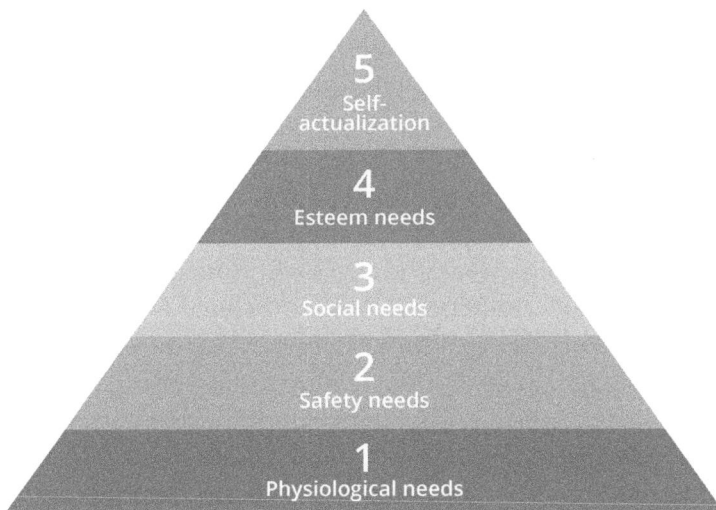

Abraham Maslow's Hierarchy of Needs

So, is the homeless beggar who lives every day in the unknown going through a strictly physical journey of survival searching for food, water and shelter? And was I more evolved and better off because I was going through a spiritual journey? Maslow's pyramid made perfect sense if I looked at it from the vantage point of one's lifetime. It was logical that one could not worry about social needs if one did not feel secure in the basic needs of survival. Those who are in war-torn countries are not backpacking around the world trying to figure out the meaning of life like a university student on a gap year. They are trying to get clean water, buy food and pay for rent.

However, if I looked at it from the soul's perspective, and know that the soul's purpose is to simply experience itself to attain *mukti*, or "freedom," then the pyramid is not sufficient. The pyramid is only one aspect of our multiple lifetimes as a soul experiencing its humanness. What if an evolved master soul made the conscious choice to reincarnate as a beggar for a humbling experience? Perhaps Maslow's pyramid of needs should be expanded to be more circular and mobile to honor the soul's desires too.

Maybe it's our Western education system and the corporatization of the world. From a young age, we are taught linearly through the concept of climbing the corporate ladder and competing for more things and better promotions. The symbol of the pyramid is the very definition of hierarchy and better or worse. We have been engrained to view the top of the pyramid as the top of the food chain and the ideal place to be.

I wasn't about to solve life. I had to accept that my mission in India was not to solve the great social injustices of the caste system. I was there to work on myself and become the most masterful version of myself. The only thing I could do was be kind and recognize the beggars on the streets as teachers. They were a daily reminder for me to trust in the unknown. Reminding me to trust that trivial matters of whether or not I had enough money or if I made the right choice to leave New York would all work out in the end.

The major takeaway from my second visit in India was to ground all the spiritual lessons I had received the first time around into practical and digestible points of action. Application was key. There was no way India would have the same enchanting thrall that swept me away the first time. That too was a kind of maya. I had to speak my feelings more clearly to myself and others. I had to be more open and compassionate to others who were newer on the path to spirituality. I had to judge others less, so as to stop judging myself. I had to stop wondering whether or not I deserved the position to teach in the ashram community. I had to let go of my idea of being the perfect teacher and having all the answers. I had to learn to be comfortable in making lots of mistakes and sharing my trials and tribulations with my students for the sake of my own evolution.

So, all this time, spirituality really was about being more truthful to myself, and living more authentically without the layers and layers of pretense. I thought it was this mystical search for blue cosmic avatars who appeared out of nowhere while meditating in the Himalayan caves for months on end. I thought in order for me to qualify as someone on a spiritual journey, I needed to find a guru and kiss their feet and be of service for many years until I ascended the ranks of discipleship and proved my devotion.

I met so many people who had these mystical stories and fantastical descriptions of getting divine messages through the language of symbols and dreams. On the flip side, they were having issues on the material plane. If they didn't have enough money and had crabby attitudes when their phones stopped working, they would blame capitalism and go on rants about injustice, declaring money as the Devil's institution. I found it all to be so silly. As far as I was concerned, they were acting like any uncharitable millionaire who hoarded riches out of entitlement. It was the opposite side of the same coin. The blame game was so tiring. I found it more fruitful to accept the reality of how things were, and to actively choose whether to stay with the status quo or break from the pack. Blaming and complaining were just angrier mutations of pity, and just as useless.

I had high hopes of finding a guru in India, only to find Swamiji telling me to be my own guru. A guru is a spiritual teacher who dispels illusion and helps to catalyze great internal shifts. Ironically, the more Swamiji reminded me that Jesus wasn't a Christian, Buddha wasn't a Buddhist and Mohammed wasn't a Muslim, the more I regarded him as my spiritual guru. When I was questioned by other seekers who my guru was, by dropping Swamiji's name I felt more substantial. It felt safe, like how you feel as a child, knowing your parents are there to make sure you don't fall. It was also a seal of approval. It seemed the natural progression of one's spiritual journey was first to be taken under the wings of a guru, then become a lifelong disciple and eventually attain enlightenment after many hours of devotion. Yet, somehow, as hard as I tried, it didn't feel like a right fit, or I was told, "No, you don't get a guru."

Slowly, over the months of being in India and coming across probing seekers who grilled me on my path, I began to own my guru-lessness more comfortably. This sense of dependence on a guru can be likened to how one worships in the temple. In India, there are thousands of deities, like the goddess of wealth, Lakshmi, or Shiva the transformer. The deities are prayed to in the hopes that the worshipper will get something in return. Some offer fruit, flowers, incense and a temple donation for more wealth or improved health. The transactional nature of Hindu temple worship reminded me of my father's Buddhist prayers over the family altar. This quality of tit for tat never resonated well with my need for self-sufficiency. It creates a codependency that I experienced as unhealthy and limiting.

However, when spiritual worship is practiced with the understanding that the deities are a reflection of qualities which are already in us, waiting to make themselves known, everything changes. Worship becomes a ritual of self-respect and self-love. It is no longer about bowing down to a supernatural unseen force that will unleash a hoard of locusts on our rice fields if we don't pay tribute. Even in the heart of the spiritual motherland, in the Himalayas, many Hindus worship from a place of separation and fear. The individual is made out to be at the mercy of the almighty gods and goddesses. But what if abundance, self-worth, transformation and love already exist within? And, through worship, which can be as simple as creating a simple ritual of remembrance, these qualities are amplified out into world? What if we bow down to our own mastery, and not our master, in the spirit of self-respect and self-love because we don't see ourselves as separate from God but rather see that we are of God? And so, we are God. In bowing down to the guru, we are actually just bowing down to a mirror of our potential to co-create our reality.

As much as I wanted to stay in India and adopt the mission of becoming the vice president of this Reiki and meditation healing center, deep down I knew it didn't reflect my most authentic truth. It was Swamiji's truth. After all, he taught me discernment and to listen to my heart. And I felt stifled in this teacher-student relationship that felt like a replication of a father-and-son relationship we had lifetimes ago. It was reminiscent of the mother-and-son obligation I felt with Courtney in New York.

I knew that in order to make a true internal shift, I had to cultivate a sense of true independence. This meant no matter how much I supported or believed in Courtney's vision or Swami Amitanand's vision, I could not be a part of these missions until I had figured out what I really wanted. Up until that point in time, all I had been doing as Courtney's manager or would be doing as Swamiji's vice president was act out an idea of what I believed my life's purpose could be. When I was around them, I covered up certain aspects of myself because I felt those parts of me were not showable. And as dear as I hold my teachers in my heart, a part of me felt as if I were living up to imagined expectations of me. I had to leave the nest and find out for myself.

Through distancing myself from my esteemed teachers, I figured out that my true purpose was not to ride on their coattails. It felt right to be my own boss and make my own rules and answer only to myself in the way I conduct my business—just as it may be someone else's truth to work for a large organization as an employee. Things were the way they were, and I ultimately had to decide if I was going to commit to my journey of self-discovery or hide in the safety of familiarity.

Years later, I learned through the Human Design System, founded by Ra Uru Hu, that my archetype was a heretical and investigative Manifestor bound to a destiny of transpersonal karma. It was comical that these were the names of the archetypes I belonged to. However, they made sense. My inquisitive rebelliousness naturally fit in with these roles. I have always had a deep desire to pierce the veil to see what's really behind the magic curtain.

I also learned that as a soul designed to experience transpersonal karma versus a fixed fate or personal destiny in my blueprint, the fulfilment of my soul's purpose would only happen if I openly used my life's journey with my tribe of spiritual seekers. Essentially, what was told to me by a Human Design expert was that my life is meant to be lived for the betterment of the collective whole. While some are designed to fulfill their personal wishes and goals by living for themselves, my success would come from service to humanity.

I was melancholic at times with these new bits of information. The uncomfortable part of myself wanted to have normal desires. A family, perhaps. A house. Maybe even getting a recurring role on a sci-fi show and playing an alien. I always loved sci-fi. As a child, I watched *Star Trek* religiously and would talk to the stars at night. Amid all the traveling and global transformational experiences I've had, this was my secret wish: to be grounded in the normality of my humanness. A huge part of that secret wish was colored by my parents' wishes and the wishes that their parents had for them—generations and generations of expectations that I have to remind myself are not my own. Hence all my seeking and absorbing of esoteric wisdom to remind me of that.

As a manifestor, I am gifted with the initiative to transform energy into action. According to Human Design, manifestors are one of four types, making up 9 percent of the entire population, and tend to operate on their own. Typically, when one encounters a manifestor type, they will feel their own aura shrinking, as we have closed and repelling auras. When a Human Design interpreter educated me about my nuanced chart, it gave so much perspective as to why I was angry all the time growing up. Though at first I saw having a closed aura as not particularly desirable, soon I realized that my closed aura served as the necessary friction to be able to question the status quo. The vehicle I was gifted with was designed to naturally provoke those who lived an unquestioned and homogenized existence. Most of my childhood and young adult life was spent trying to fit in, but I was never meant to fit in and always remained in the periphery, living as an outcast because I was designed to be an outcast.

Way before being introduced to my Human Design analysis, I arrived at this point intuitively by making so many mistakes through my working relationships and different projects that I endeavored to complete. Lo and behold, this logical empirical system that described how I was designed to function affirmed what I discovered along the way. All my spiritual teachers simply guided me to quiet the mind and listen to my heart, and it offered the same conclusion as this new bit of information. However, the Human Design analysis did satiate the logical part of my brain that is so fond of rationalizing.

Ra Uru Hu uses the metaphor that "the Human Design chart is our Vehicle and it comes in with its own driver. The Personality is the Passenger and it sits in the back seat." It was such the perfect metaphor for how most of us live trying to run from destiny and end up as disgruntled backseat drivers who just don't get our way. Our minds, which are polluted with conditioned programs from our fear-based societies, start infecting the passenger in the back seat with untruths: That we were only born to work hard and follow somebody else's set of rules. That we are not worthy. That we should not live our dreams. That we are not loveable—and a whole plethora of unuseful thoughts that spoil the quality of our lives.

The irony is that without coming into this world with bags of issues, life would be boring. If we change our perspective and see our problems as opportunities to grow, then we, as the passenger in the vehicle of life, can enjoy the ride because we know when to back down and when to step out into the limelight.

When my six months was nearly up at Anand Prakash Ashram, I listened to that call that said "Don't go back; go forward into the unknown, and amazing things will happen." I didn't need to live out this story of volunteering and being flat broke for another six months or five years until I accumulated the sufficient quota of hours to be labeled as someone deserving the title of a true seeker. Who was I trying to impress, anyway?

Through meditation, I figured out that I honestly could not stay in India past my original six-month plan. Staying any longer would mean denying the aspect of myself that yearned for luxury and comfort.

One of the most important lessons I learned through all my seeking is that it is not wrong to have an appreciation for the finer things in life. Spirituality and materialism go hand in hand. Not feeling bad about it was a huge breakthrough. This was how I was going to authentically live my truth. While I met some amazing people who devoted years and years of service to their gurus and their own spiritual processes, for me to grow, I had to obliterate any idea of needing to go through someone else's ring of fire.

And so I made the decision to separate from my precious India. Teaching opportunities presented themselves in Hong Kong, Sydney and Singapore, and without even knowing where Singapore was on the map, I made a decision and started a whole new chapter of self-discovery on that little red dot in the middle of Southeast Asia.

CHAPTER 13

SINGAPORE: TRANSMUTING KARMA

ॐ

"Karma is inherited from the past and affects the future. Dharma neutralizes karma and brings us into the present moment."

JOHNSON CHONG

At the end of the day, I am a city kid at heart. I was born and raised in New York City, so I inherently understood city people. Simultaneously, I understood the importance of nature and developed an appreciation for simple living in India. Even knowing this juxtaposition, I still surprised myself by going from rural India to the most expensive country in the world.

Well before I even knew where Singapore was on the map, Courtney had a dream about me driving a bus full of Asian people. The synchronicities between our dream worlds and how the symbols and stories translate into real life are sometimes unbelievable. We had an inexplicable relationship on a soul level. When Vlad, my psychic and divine healer friend, told me he had a similar dream, I flagged it as a foreshadowing of future events that would unfold in completely unexpected ways.

What this eventually led to was six years of living in Singapore. I have had the great fortune of leading spiritual retreats around Southeast Asia and creating Sagehouse, a studio for conscious movement, meditation and healing. So the metaphor of driving a bus full of Asian people was about me coming into my own as a leader of spirituality in Asia.

One of the most pleasant surprises was that I came into a relationship with my current partner most unexpectedly. I surrendered any idea of wanting what I thought I deserved, and what I no longer obsessed over naturally came to be. For the majority of my twenties, I longed to be in a loving romantic relationship because I thought it would help heal the wounds from my conservative, repressed upbringing. I was so sexually repressed and scared that I never dared to experiment with drugs, alcohol or even dating when I was in high school. So my twenties erupted into a desperate need to be loved and to love, out of a fear of feeling left behind.

As potent and valid as the law of attraction is in self-development and spiritual development communities around the world, I would love to say I actively attracted this into my life, but I didn't, per se. This philosophy states that focusing on positive or negative thoughts can manifest positive or negative experiences in one's life consciously or unconsciously. Instead, I dropped all expectations I had about who I should and should not meet and surrendered to the experience of being open to new people and experiences. And because I was more aligned to my highest purpose after leaving India than I was in the chaos of New York, a new lover appeared. With all the internal work that I had been doing, I was ready to be loved and to love without old fears initiating it.

I met Andy online, as most gay men do in this digital age—for the sake of convenience and because it sometimes feels more manageable and emotionally safer behind the protection of a screen. Some of my previous relationships were also through the internet, and some were not. The difference this time around was that I dropped all expectations of the "ideal" I thought I deserved. Most of that ideal was an illusory romantic notion conditioned by straight, cookie-cutter Hollywood rom-coms anyway, so it didn't make actual sense in my reality. As a result, I met someone who I never thought would be my type—someone who was such the opposite of me that it enhanced my life in ways I never thought it would. His pragmatism grounded me, and my spirituality elevated him.

The yogic understanding of thoughts as energy patterns is very real. Even modern science, through the field of quantum physics, has reaffirmed how our reality is co-created by the quality of our thoughts. Thoughts are merely energy patterns in need of direction. That direction is ultimately up to us to choose. Do we suffer at the whims of chaotic experience, or do we transmute chaos to order?

In my twenties, when I unconsciously held onto the emotional stories that kept me in a defeated relationship with my inner self-saboteur, I attracted those types of relationships into my romantic life. Through my coming out to my parents and deconditioning my longing for the "ideal" family and accepting that my story was never going to be the ideal, my energy field changed. It was no longer clouded with the neediness of a wounded child that desperately sought to be held because he was hurt. Swamiji would talk about it in terms of energy spilling from the solar plexus and others talked about patching up holes in the auric field, while some shamans I encountered explained it in terms of the rainbow light body.

Everyone was saying the same thing. The difference in how I moved through my life in my twenties versus now in my thirties can be allegorized as me starting out carrying my family's, ancestor's, and society's suitcases of expectations around with me, and then transitioning to just carrying my suitcase. The next step would be to carry no suitcase, but I'm not there yet.

The emotional baggage metaphor can be equated to the Hindu and Buddhist concepts of karma and dharma. Our ever-growing awareness of these forces is integral to our spiritual evolution. We can look at karma as the laws of cause and effect and dharma as the laws of the universe, which can come across as very intimidating and not as digestible when trying to apply it to our lives.

From my personal experiences and realizations of how karma plays out in my life, karma is the cycle of giving and receiving. Simply put, the kind of thoughts, words or actions we offer the world will be returned in full to us one way or another. Our attachments to only what is pleasurable or not pleasurable color how we see karma, as in the ancient Hindu caste systems that delineate karma as good or bad. I don't see karma as having these human limitations. Karma itself is neutral. Good and bad is something that religion colors over an experience we have, to create guilt for the sake of controlling the masses.

In my rebellious days as a teenager, I shoplifted from big chain stores and never got caught. However, in the natural order of things, I did not get away scot-free without giving something in return. I would lose money from my wallet or get a parking ticket worth the same value as what I had willfully taken. It not only worked out on the physical plane. This played out in my thought patterns too. In college, when I waited tables in Times Square, we got lots of tourists from the South. The ongoing generalization was that Southerners were bad tippers. An automated suggested service charge was put on the bills after 6 PM. Sometimes, unsuspecting customers would not notice it and tip on top of the suggested service charge. Every waiter saw this act of hustling as a good night. By not being transparent and letting our guests know beforehand, and hoping they would not read the fine print, me and my waiters created an energy field of greed. This would infect the whole of the next shift. Like clockwork, during the next shift, I would find myself with an entire section of frustratingly low-tipping and difficult patrons. Then, on the days when I completely let go of my preconceived notions of who might or might not tip well, I always found myself pleasantly surprised when collecting the bill. Karma is not all about physical action; thoughts and words are just as significant in creating a karmic loop.

Across Hinduism, Buddhism, Jainism and Sikhism, dharma is expressed in many ways and can get rather confusing and theologically verbose. I experience karma as the web that keeps duality alive—like good and bad, right and wrong, a.k.a. the conditions and programming that have kept us from living as our true selves. Dharma is the way out of this cycle. And it is essentially a choice we have to make individually. Have we had enough of playing by everyone else's rules? Do we want to step into our birthright of embodying peace, love and joy unconditionally?

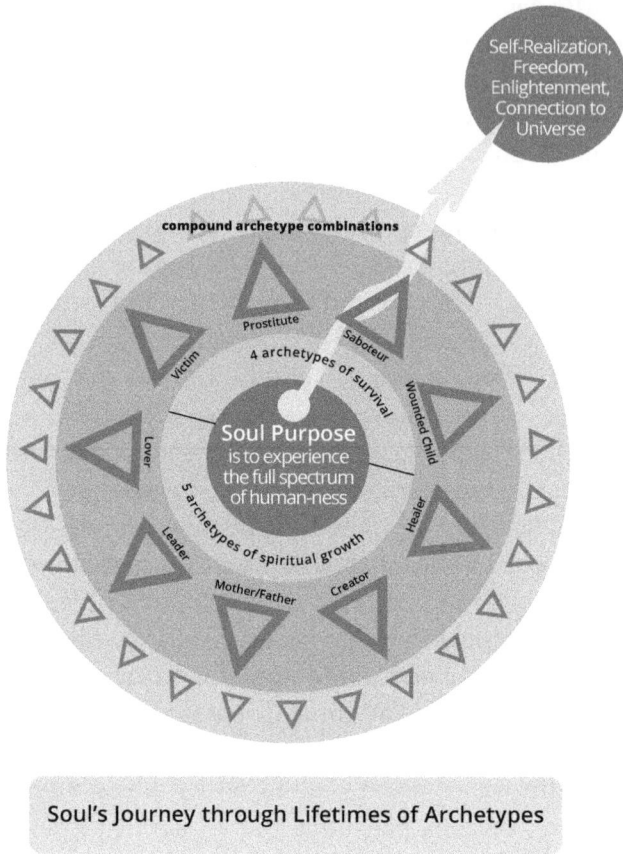

Soul's Journey through Lifetimes of Archetypes

Fig 4. My diagram of the soul's journey through lifetimes of archetypes—We all enter this life wounded by the need to survive and layers of conditioned generational programs passed onto us by our parents. Our soul then seeks to experience these archetypal patterns for the purpose of experiencing itself— everything from pain to joy. When we come to realize the repetitive patterns and are exhausted by the hamster wheel of human experiences, we begin the process of aligning with our dharma, to break free of the loop. It is here where our infinite potential exists and where everything beyond our wildest dreams is possible.

Dharma is difficult to translate and has many meanings throughout various ancient translations of spiritual texts. We can look at dharma as the duties and responsibilities given to us to complete during this lifetime. Another word for it would be our *purpose*. It's our original contract that we created before we were born, which contains the blueprint of experiences we signed up for during this incarnation. Of course, the density of the karmic loop affects how graceful or not graceful we will be when finding our own unique way.

My mini-awakening experiences—starting in university, until I arrived in India for the second time—were pivotal in setting me up to accept my dharma. If I had not spent a year drifting at SUNY Geneseo, confused about my future, studying a mishmash of random subjects, I would not have had my first conscious experience of divine intervention. That experience then led me to meet the exact people I needed to meet in the acting conservatory in order to acquire the mental and emotional tools I needed to be who I am today.

It just so happened that the year I entered my program, the conservatory decided to experiment with a more mind-body-based training program through Alexander, Feldenkrais, clown work, and many other somatic-inquiry-based models of movement, on top of all the acting training. Many people in my class and the upperclassmen would remark how we received less acting training than the classes above us and the classes below us. The faculty was constantly rotating, and professors were coming in and out. But that particular combination of teachers at that specific point in time catalyzed a deep connection to my kinesthetic and emotional intelligence.

This development strengthened my physical body so that it could contain and process the energies I would experience through later spiritual experiences. And, being more on the introverted spectrum in high school, theatre was a way for me to escape from reality. Acting school helped me transform the escapism aspect I was enamored with into an experience where I was embodying my truth via the life of another character. It was a constant exploration of human psychology and living the human experience through the thoughts, words and actions of someone else, only to realize that I shared the same need to be loved and to love. It was the fundamental basis of every character, whether they were the protagonist or the antagonist of the story.

There were many natural moments of great expansion and contraction—feelings of moving forward and taking many steps backward. It was an emotional rollercoaster ride and continues to be. I had to learn to discern the difference between dreams and fantasy. After our East Coast and West Coast acting showcases, the reality was that the agencies in LA were not as open to me as the ones in NY. One of my showcase scenes involved playing a hardcore interrogator, and in the other scene I stepped outside the box and did something drastic. I played a transvestite who was teaching her protégé how to turn tricks. Some thought it was a bad choice, and some remarked that it was a brave choice, but it ultimately confused casting directors' opinion of me, so I was deemed too weird to cast at the time. My high hopes of moving to LA and auditioning for sci-fi shows seemed remote after the showcase.

I call it fantasy because my scene choices were not in alignment with the truest expression of who I was. They were chosen with the agenda to challenge and to seek approval. Also, I figured out my desire to relocate to LA was based on avoiding the lumbering real issues with my parents: the emotional stories of rejection from a wounded childhood. At the end of the day, it was an escape tactic.

I ended up in Montgomery, Alabama, at the Shakespeare Festival as an apprentice company member. During those nine slow months, I took up teaching community yoga classes to a group of ladies I met at the YMCA who repeatedly asked me to. The seed of teaching was planted. As a result, I returned to New York attending workshops and trainings in yoga, Thai massage, Pilates, meditation and attending spiritual events with eye-opening teachers. All of this prepared me for my coming out to my parents and the massive release of my perceived identity as an actor and all the expectations I unconsciously placed on myself through the pressures of family while I was in India. After two years in Singapore, I realized that every experience in my life led me to the path that I was on. My dharma.

When I arrived in Singapore, I felt so out of place and wanted to go back to India. There was a stuffiness and rigidity to how people followed the rules that annoyed me. It was a stark contrast to the alluring chaos of India. Chinese Singaporeans reminded me of a mutated variation of my parents. Under the mix of cultures and the unusual hybrid of dialectal accents that is the Singaporean sound, I felt the restraint of Chinese culture infringing on the free expression of most locals I met. It was so very different from the artistic community of friends I had back home and the lively soul searchers I encountered in India. The fancy buildings, the shopping malls and the glitz of wealthy living had no appeal to me, so Singapore felt dry and lackluster in comparison.

Why was I here? It felt like the time I so badly wanted to be in *Arabian Nights* by Mary Zimmerman at Berkeley Repertory Theatre and ended up in Alabama doing Shakespeare instead. Or when I wanted to be in *American Night* at the Denver Center, but ended up doing *The Piano Teacher* at Cincinnati Playhouse. I had a history of wanting to be somewhere other than where I was, and I was determined to get to the bottom of it.

I had a brilliant teaching assignment. Seventeen hours a week at a yoga studio. I tried to tie in spiritual concepts to the physical classes with little interest from the overall population of students. But it was well paid, and I had a living stipend and plenty of cash to live comfortably. My friend from New York introduced me to our now-mutual friend, Stephanie, my only friend at the time. I spent my first month completely bewildered. Why did I leave India and trade New York City for this puzzling place? That seemed to be the question that most people asked me. "Why would you ever leave New York?" I always said I left because I had enough of the madness but really wanted to blurt out, "To free myself from the micromanagement of my parents."

I was definitely an enigma. I looked like I could be from Singapore, yet I had no roots or existing family in Singapore. I felt compelled to explore the acting scene in Asia and went off to one of the oldest and most influential talent agencies in Singapore to discuss representation. I was told that I could not be represented because I did not fit in with the locals. Apparently, I was too green in Singapore and did not understand the culture enough to be castable. In plain words, they told me I presented too white as an Asian by the way I spoke. I was stunned. Wasn't acting about creating stories through building characters? I was suddenly reminded what I hated most about the industry, the judgmental hocus-pocus that goes on during the casting process.

In the States, it was bad practice for a casting director to ask your age. But in Singapore, it was mandatory to fill out your age on the forms. And, at twenty-eight years old, I was being sent out for casting calls for young fathers. I had a feeling it was a government initiative to excite the young people to start another baby boom. Did I give off dad vibes? It was bizarre. Stateside, it was about not being Asian enough for TV jobs. I was apparently too tall and too well polished to fit the stereotype of the nerdy math genius, IT wizard, or Chinese delivery guy. The entertainment industry in Singapore was a different strain of the same virus. It was the universe challenging me to see if I wanted to put up with the same crap in a brand-new environment. Because I had all this time on my hands, I started to do student films for fun, and submitted myself for Shakespeare in the Park with Singapore Repertory Theatre. I figured anyone doing Shakespeare would be more open and colorblind in their casting than the more legit and commercial avenues of the entertainment industry.

I gave Singapore a three-month trial and ended up staying for six months on top of that to play Lorenzo in *The Merchant of Venice* with Singapore Repertory Theatre. During that time of intense internal reevaluation of what I truly wanted, I reaffirmed for myself that the erratic life of a performer definitely was not it. Though I had an amazing time with Shakespeare, the nomadic instability of a performer's life was too unsettling. I needed serious grounding. Meeting Andy was part of the grounding experience I needed.

Astrologers talk about our fated Saturn return. The planet that is responsible for the law of karma, Saturn highlights the lessons we are meant to learn in this lifetime and our karmic contract from previous incarnations. It takes Saturn about 29.5 years to return to the position it held at the time of our births. This means between the ages of twenty-eight and thirty-one, everyone will go through a metaphorical rebirth. And at this pivotal juncture, we all start to question who we are and what we really want out of life. The second time we experience our Saturn return is from our mid-fifties to sixty, when most people arrive at what we know as the "midlife crisis."

Every time Saturn returns, we are given the choice of either repeating the same physical, mental, emotional and energetic patterns that we have repeated for lifetimes or waking up from that slumber and moving forward into a new experience, into the unknown. When we resist our greater and unknown purpose, we can experience a very bumpy ride. In flowing with life and arriving at a place I did not initially understand, my Saturn return was quite liberating and fluid.

I was living a very different life in Singapore. I met a different group of friends that I would have never met in New York. I hopped from my artist tribe to being surrounded by financially savvy and jet-setter types. I was able to travel and lead retreats to exotic locations that I never imagined would be possible living on the other side of the globe. I led retreats in places like Malaysia, Greece, Bali, India, Thailand, Nepal, and my favorite so far, Bhutan. The prophecy of Sri Ma Amodini saying that my life was meant to be full of travel was coming true.

I don't attribute any of this to luck or being more fortunate than others. I see this as the constant practice of expanding my awareness—noticing my habits and patterns, the ways in which I choose to do things or not do things, and questioning why. Through this process of self-inquiry, I usually arrive at a realization that turns my world upside down, a new chapter of self-discovery and reinvention.

It really is exciting. And it takes a great deal of faith to leap into the unknown. Each time I arrive on the other side, what I discover is always surprising. Instead of fearing the newness and clinging to the comfort of what I already have, I instead think, *Wow, this is actually awesome. I'm so fortunate to have gotten here.* Here I am, living in Southeast Asia where the apartment experience is nowhere compared to New York where you get a shoebox for way too much rent. I have lived in spacious condos with Olympic-sized pools, a beautiful Peranakan conservation shophouse, and have been able to afford traveling and doing the things that fuel my life purpose. Compared to the angst-y and confused mid-twenties version of me, my life is so much more amazing than I could have imagined it to be.

None of this could have happened without my willingness to become aware of the years of karma that I had created unconsciously for myself, and then releasing the karmic stories that kept me tied to unrealistic expectations.

CHAPTER 14

DISCOVERING GIFTS FROM MY ANCESTORS

*"Even though they had forgotten who they were,
somewhere inside of them, the gift of their ancestors remained."*

GREGG BRADEN

When I was four or five years old, I tried to pick up a bowling ball but instead dropped it on my father's right big toe. It bounced off of his toe onto my left big toe. We have two mirrored cracks on our big toes, and our nails have always grown back with a split down the middle. I will never forget his expression of anger over my childlike ignorance of my limits mixed with his howling screams of agony. I cried and cried for what seemed like hours as the chaos of my mother trying to quell the situation made things worse. Being the brilliant multitasker, she managed to reprimand me for my playfulness and accuse my father of not being attentive, while at the same time icing our black-and-blue toes. In the spiritual world, there are no such things as accidents. And little did I know at the time, but this connection between my father and I stemmed from a long line of pain and suffering from our ancestral lineage.

The toenail crack wasn't the only common physical affliction we suffered. We both have a physical block on our right rotator cuffs that doesn't permit our right arms to be placed in the "under arrest" position like our left arms. I discovered the adhesion while doing bodywork on my dad several years ago when he was experiencing tightness around his chest and shoulders.

Despite our many differences, he still called on me for help when needed, and I helped when I was able. During that time, my father had a heart scare, as his three older brothers all had heart-related issues, and one of my uncles even died from heart disease. He cut down massively on his meat intake and made a decision to become more devout in chanting Buddhist prayers in the name of longevity. In the same vein of multitasking like my mother, he also prayed for grandchildren and a miracle to turn me from my unorthodox ways.

My father was always disciplined in routine and found great solace in structure. When I was younger, he got up before driving us to school to do his qigong exercises, which fell to the wayside over the years. Amusingly, after I came out to them, his qigong practice evolved into a daily practice of chanting and prayer instead.

I don't agree with his agenda when praying to Gwan Yin, the goddess of compassion. Nonetheless, a part of me was content to know that he readopted a spiritual discipline into his routine. At least the chanting helped him to cope with his anxiety and frustrations about what he could and could not control in life. The onus was on me to either embrace his newfound spirituality as a step in the right direction. Or would I get annoyed by it and allow it to create more friction between us?

Whenever I touch a physical body and am tuned in with the focus of clearing and releasing, I receive information either in images and emotions, or I get a sense of deeply knowing something. The body chronicles the full range of human experiences from the heights of happiness to the depths of darkness. While working on his shoulder, I felt the recorded history of pain that was surfacing. These traffic jams in his physical body were manifestations of the stories that bound my father in a karmic loop indebted to his ancestral lineage.

The eight years he floated from his home village and Guangdong City trying to escape the mainland into Macau or Hong Kong, he was beaten, bound and jailed five times. He worked various odd jobs until he saved up enough money to pay his way on the cargo hold of any boat brave enough to ferry him across. Five times he failed. And five times he was caught.

During these periods of captivity, the city authorities would ask which home village he belonged to with the intention of sending him back to be dealt with by the local authorities. Knowing his fate, each time he attempted to prolong his stay in the Guangzhou City jail by incorrectly naming where he was from. He was much safer there than in the hands of an angry town council waiting to bludgeon him to death. They would take a few days or weeks to verify if he was registered with that village. He would sit in jail with a bowl of rice a day to eat, and from time to time snack on insects he found crawling up and down the walls.

He sustained injuries to his right shoulder and recounted that it felt like his arm was going to break off during times of great physical struggle with his guards. This was a huge piece of information for me. I had not gone through these traumatic experiences, yet the physical injuries that he sustained were somehow mirrored in my body. It gave "family curse" a whole new dimension. The transference of this imprint via my father's life story had rubbed off physically, mentally, emotionally and energetically on me. As a result, my physical body carried the battle scars of my father's history that burdened his shoulders. I later discovered in my visits to China that this history of suffering was not limited to my father, but rather expanded throughout our bloodline in permutations of betrayal, abuse, abandonment, rejection and lots and lots of violence.

The decision of whether I wanted to resign to this ill-fated cycle of karmic conflict and suffering or flip the switch and play a different game altogether was ultimately my own. I chose the latter—the more conscious and difficult path. This meant digging deep into the shadows and redefining my relationship with all these family stories.

The first time I went to China was when I was twenty-four years old. My father, mother and brother had gone two years prior to me going. I had an important showcase for acting agents in New York and LA then and opted not to go. The three weeks I went back with my mother to her hometown of Tai San was full of agitation. Back then, I was not emotionally mature enough to accept my mother's pitfalls with ease and grace. I still scrutinized her worldviews and belief systems as archaic. And I judged everything and everyone around her with a penetrating air of "I'm more conscious than you; therefore, I'm better than you."

My mother's second-eldest brother's daughter was getting married, and my uncle wanted to do a Ching Ming ceremony to create a stream of auspicious energy for the Lee family. Ching Ming is a traditional ancestral tomb-sweeping festival observed around the spring equinox, where certain ceremonial rites and prayers are offered to honor and memorialize the dead.

I was four years into my vegetarianism, abiding by the yogic principle of *ahimsa*, "nonviolence," and I felt very strongly about exploitative killing. This was a bout of contention between me and my uncle—my traditional, Chinese-massage-therapist uncle who criticized my Thai massage training and thought me unmanly for eating only vegetables. He was so bothered by my eccentricities that he took me out on a man-up day.

In a strange fatherly way, he left my mom and aunt to go shopping and signaled me to follow him. A cigarette hanging from his mouth, in his smoker's rasp he simply asked, "You wanna eat?" *Sure*, I thought. Anything to get away from my overbearing mother, who seemed to be on the lookout for a domesticated girl with a sizeable dowry for her "unique" son. All of her friends wanted to know just how single I was, and when I was getting married.

I left without a second to think and found myself in a restaurant that served cat meat. My uncle urged me to give cat a try. I watched him devour his plate of cat, as I nauseously ate my plate of tofu and mixed vegetables. He wasn't a man of many words, plus there wasn't much to talk about, so he got up and commanded me to go get a massage with him. I suddenly found myself in a less-than-reputable massage establishment staffed with girls who looked like they were out of a *Hello Kitty* call-girl magazine. It was as if he was surveying my every action and reaction around these girls. Needless to say, I had a bizarre day where my uncle and I barely exchanged words on account of how uncomfortable we both were to be tiptoeing around each other.

So, when he exploded at me in the most vocal of ways when I refused to carry the dead pig up the mountains for the tomb-sweeping ceremony, I was not at all surprised. There was this unspoken air of fundamental disagreement between us. I found the whole thing primitive and superstitious, and he saw it as the pinnacle of manly duty and responsibility.

My mom and uncle had hired these villagers to help with the ceremony, and everyone stared at me as this strange enigma. My New-York-isms were not impressive in the echoes of communist obedience. I stood my ground and fiercely replied, "You killed it, so you bring it up. I'm not doing it." They killed this grown pig, speared it with a pole from mouth to tail, and barbequed it until it was bright red. The facial expression of the pig was one of sheer horror. It had become the color of burnt skin and looked as if it were scorched alive. I wanted to take no part in this barbaric ritual, and I grudgingly trailed behind the whole-day procession of villagers and family to the gravesites.

At the end of eight hours of walking up and down different hills and mountains to pay our respects, they carried the pig back to my mother's childhood home. Then they laid out a spread of newspaper on the floor, un-skewered the pig, hacked it to bits and ate it.

If I had to compare my mother's hometown to an American equivalent, it would be the Asian parallel of a small rural mountain community in Appalachia. They were people of the earth, bound by customs and traditions.

My snobbery and contempt for being a part of this family exponentially added to the self-shame I was already feeling. I could not reconcile the cultural differences of Western individualism and the expectations of Eastern familial obligation. Why did my soul choose to reincarnate into this culture?

Before the week was over, my mother and I visited my father's village of Yangjiang, two hours away by car to see where he grew up. His hometown had a very different vibe as it was a coastal village. Since he could not make it with us this time around, I didn't get the full picture. It was meant to be, because what was meant to happen happened nine years later when I turned thirty-three and not when I was a judgmental, unripe twenty-four-year-old.

In December of 2008, my father's third-eldest brother was murdered. My dad always felt uneasy and helpless about the entire situation. I think, in a way, he always blamed himself for leaving his brothers behind in Hong Kong and Macau. And he thought that by his breaking off from the family, the unfortunate demise of his brother was his fault.

My father is the youngest of five. Before the Cultural Revolution, his father met with disaster when he slipped and suffered a deadly concussion on his daily round of collecting firewood to feed the family. My paternal grandmother gave away my aunt to my grand-aunt because they couldn't afford to raise her, and she also sold my father to a family who couldn't have children. Enraged, my eldest uncle took it upon himself to find my father, and eventually brought him home.

During the Cultural Revolution from 1966 to 1976, Mao Zedong segregated groups of people into five black categories of enemies of the state. He turned family members on each other, and those who fell into the black categories were weeded out for public humiliation, reeducation and beatings. The men in my family fell under the first category of landlords. As a result, they suffered the worst kind of degradation and persecution. The Communist Party victimized my father and his family to push the propaganda of glorifying Mao as this benevolent leader and visionary for the people.

One day, my father came home and found his mother murdered in the bedroom they shared. She was hanged from the ceiling. This staged suicide was the beginning of my father's epic journey that eventually brought him to America. His brothers had already fled to Hong Kong and Macau in earlier years, but my dad opted to stay behind to care for his aging mother. The day he turned sixteen, his maternal uncle helped him escape his village before other relatives could turn on him. This was the day my father's already deep wounds of rejection and abandonment were even more deeply etched into his being. Not only had his country betrayed him, but family members turned on him out of fear for their own livelihood.

My mother's sister was working at my paternal-uncle-number-three's rubber factory in Hong Kong. The connections were made, and my father and mother soon found each other, escaping with four others on an underground railroad of sorts away from persecution. After eight days and nights of hiding in the dark corners of thick jungle and unmarked paths, they swam to safety from Shenzhen to Hong Kong, which was under British rule at the time.

When my mother came to America under Jimmy Carter's 1980 Refugee Act that offered admission to people under persecution from their homeland, my father stayed behind. He could have stayed with his brothers in Hong Kong and Macau, but the fear of being taken by the Communist Party always loomed over his head. His brothers had entered legally before the Cultural Revolution, so his only choice was to follow my mother to the States three years later.

My mother's siblings all relocated to the States, but my father was the lone wolf who left his family behind in pursuit of a better life. He would not return to Asia until 2002 when his second-eldest brother died of a heart condition. And since then, he has always been torn by the rejection from his birth country and reluctantly leaving his siblings behind.

My third uncle was successful with his rubber factory. He had four children. He had an affair with a woman who was an aspiring social climber from Sichuan. Eventually, he left his wife for her and started a second family. He was murdered in his factory in December of 2008. I remember the day I got the call from my brother when I was still performing at the Alabama Shakespeare Festival.

Dad was in the worst state I had ever seen him. I could feel guilt and helplessness ooze from him. He flew back to visit his grieving family immediately. The killer was still at large, the case left unsolved.

Two years later, he was still unsettled by the entire situation and the lack of clarity from the local authorities. His sense of justice and retribution beckoned him to return and get to the bottom of the situation. My mother and I were unable to dissuade my father. So I appealed to his spiritual authority. Chinese people are brought up honoring the spirits of the dead, so I told him I would check with Uncle's spirit if he should go back to sort things out.

I asked my friend Vlad, a psychic and realized healer from Brooklyn who was renting space from us at Studio Anya. He wasn't openly practicing mediumship anymore, as he was working as a medical intuitive, helping those diagnosed with terminal illnesses recover through his method of divine healing. He came to mind right away as I remembered the stories he told of him helping detectives locate missing bodies by supplying them with coordinates and other extraordinary tales of mediumship. He was tough but loveable and always looked at me with this sparkle in his eye like he knew exactly what I was thinking.

I sat in the yoga room with him as he created the space to bridge the gaps between the two worlds. There was no ritual or any mystical hocus-pocus about what he was doing. There was an intensity in his eyes as he stared out across the room. His eyes had the look of a mad man looking into the worlds of the unseen. He barely blinked. A moist coat layered the whites of his eyes as they bulged out of his sockets.

This was the real deal. No crystal balls involved or tarot cards needed. Vlad had a knowingness about him that superseded any other intuitive that I had ever met. He knew very specific details from connecting to a higher power, and surprised me at every turn when I thought he could astonish me no further.

Before I could lay out the details, he explained that he would ask me a series of yes or no questions so that he could differentiate the soul that would be coming to communicate with him. All he knew was that my uncle was murdered, and I was trying to help my father gain clarity from the other side.

Vlad started with a screening process. A line-up of different murdered souls showed up. He asked me if my uncle was murdered by drowning. "Was he pushed out of a building?" No and no. He had opened a potent portal, and souls with unfinished business were coming to see him. Then he said, "Was your uncle bludgeoned on the left side of his head and stabbed in the back of his neck with multiple knife wounds?" And I said yes. I was stunned by the accuracy.

He spent a few moments homing in on that particular soul. Even though my uncle didn't understand English and spoke Chinese, time and language functioned fluidly outside of our physical reality. Knowingness trumped any language barrier, and Vlad was connecting from a place beyond the five senses. Without knowing the story, he told me that my uncle was attacked from behind in the factory where he worked. He described the location and surroundings and said there were two people involved in the murder. These men were apparently looking to acquire his ledger and will. He mentioned the involvement of a woman who had two children, which I figured was my uncle's mistress-turned-wife.

My uncle had five children from his first marriage. My cousins were deleted from the will, and the family assets were redistributed to his new family. Nobody in my family liked to talk about the woman from Sichuan who snaked her way into my uncle's life. And though the news of her as the initiator of such a cruel act was appalling, I understood it to be the unconscious reenactment of my family's unprocessed ancestral karma. The stories that my family hides out of embarrassment and shame were repeated as misfortunes over and over again throughout history because the lessons had not been learned. The karma had not yet been transformed.

Vlad warned my father to stay out of the investigation and to leave it unsolved. It was gang related, and any engagement in unveiling the truth would result in more violence. Before the session was over, Vlad also asked me who "Fei Jai" was. That was a Chinese nickname meaning "Fat Boy" or "Fatty." Just before we closed, another soul had entered with a message. The cousin I had never met, my uncle's firstborn who died at a young age from a heroin overdose, came to assure me that he had passed over, and to apologize for messing up. He was involved in a lot of seedy gang-related activities and was floating around in limbo. Vlad helped to transition the two souls to the well of souls for their next embodiment assignments and assured me that all was well on that front.

I reported this experience back to my father to steer him away from getting entangled in the drama of solving the crime and ensure the safe passage of his brother's soul to the next world. It took him some time, but he eventually let go of his anger and indignation toward this great injustice that happened to his family. And it was the power of repetitive mantra and Buddhist prayer that grounded him.

During the time of my uncle's doomed fate, his youngest son, my cousin Eddie, started receiving visions and seeing the unseen, while my brother had a dark cloud of energy following him for months. The two of them have had mirrored experiences of not having things easily come in life. At the time, I was not having such visual experiences in the world of the unseen, even though I always felt an invisible thread of divine support guiding me along.

The pieces of the family puzzle came together when my cousin Jennifer took up feng shui seriously and decided it was imperative to do another Ching Ming ceremony. Traditionally, people honor the dead during Ching Ming once a year, while my family seemed to have an irregular pattern that revolved around how convenient it was.

Out of the dozens of paternal cousins I have spread across the mainland, Hong Kong and Macau, only four of us, including my father, carried out the Ching Ming rites during Easter weekend in the spring of 2018. What timing! On the Christian calendar, it was the day of Jesus's resurrection, and here I was on a short trip to China to pay my respects to the dead with my father for the first time.

My friend Mikael happened to have an assortment of sound equipment he needed help collecting from Hong Kong, which created a serendipitous opportunity for great healing. I was given permission to use his Tibetan bells, crystal singing bowls, and other instruments during the ancestral rites. On the six-hour bus ride from Hong Kong to China, my father, my cousins and I connected in a completely different way. We openly talked about the dark chapters in our family's history that everyone else seemed to avoid, and I felt an unspoken bond between my father and me that transcended our personal perceptions of gender roles and sexuality.

We had a soul mission together that existed way before our time together on this Earth, and we now had the great opportunity to help our family transmute the karma that had been unconsciously passed down from generation to generation.

Upon arrival to Yangjiang, I was introduced to an army of second cousins. Relative after relative, it was hard to keep track of how I was related to each person. They showed me the Chong family tree that was formally printed by our clan association, which connected me eighteen generations back to judges and ministers. The foreword of the family tree connected us to King Zhuang of Chu who was a monarch of the Zhou dynasty from 613 to 591 BC. It also connected our family lineage to the creators of the compass during the first and second century.

How accurate this all is, I don't know. But then again, I've learned that the truth is subjective, and if the members of the Chong clan are empowered by feeling this ancient kinship to royalty and the ancient geomancers and fortunetellers, then who am I to question and doubt that? Growing up without the circle of a large extended family and grandparents left me feeling very disconnected from this sense of tribe that is inherently a part of Chinese culture. These new bits of information enhanced the clarity of my soul's mission and how I was designed to serve and guide others to arrive at their own spiritual clarity.

We awoke early Sunday morning to head out to the lands where my ancestors were buried. It was a good sign that the oxen on the rice paddy fields were not flaring their snouts at me ready to charge their powerful horns into my flesh like they did nine years earlier. I was different. I didn't carry that pretentious air of snobbery over my family and the ancestral homeland. Even the geese squawked a welcoming tune for what was about to happen.

The cakes, pies and scorched red pig came out of the truck, and we marched our way up the hills and valleys, starting our ancestral rites with our great-great-great-grandfather and grandmother five generations back. During the course of the day, we moved through eight different tombstones. Each burial site had a specific resonance about them. Some grave sites were about honoring and paying respects, while some were about clearing and assisting lingering remnants of confused souls to the other side.

My village relatives accepted the unfamiliar foreign ritual offerings I added to their traditional customs. Jennifer and Eddie helped to sage the grounds and ring the Tibetan bells, while my father took an instant liking to Mikael's rattle and integrated his fervent Buddhist chants with the sounds of his new shamanic shaker. I offered prayers in the form of archetypal sounds and healing mantras while sounding the crystal singing bowls. My village relatives presented their offerings and prayers in the known traditional ways. It was a marriage of the old and the new, a meeting of the conventional and the unusual. We spent on average twenty to thirty minutes in each area creating new rituals uniquely for the moment, never to be repeated the same way again.

At one grave site, I instantly knew there was something amiss with how my great-grandmother was treated during her lifetime. I felt her story of rejection and being an outcast flood my body in a way I cannot explain in words. Being that my Chinese reading skills were not up to snuff, Eddie told me that our great-grandmother's name engraved on the tombstone was the equivalent of "Jane Doe" in English. No one in our family, even our village relatives, seemed to know her given name or from which village she came. Two and two came together, and I knew this was my other connection. Two years earlier, my sister and I sent a DNA ancestry saliva test back to the lab out of curiosity and discovered we were 12 percent Dai (which is an ethnic minority connected to Thailand and Laos). And though there is no way to exactly know where it came from, I had a strong intuition it was related to my great-grandmother Jane Doe.

During another ancestral rite, I received flashes of unsettledness and a sense of great injustice. I asked my relatives what had happened to this particular great-grandfather. The response was, "This one fell off the mountain and died because a feng shui master cursed him." It seemed the fatalistic theme of being the subject of a curse stemmed farther back than my grandfather's time, who also "fell off the mountain" and suffered a deadly concussion.

There were so many storylines and themes that came out of being present with the land. I didn't focus or tune in to the details, but instead listened to the themes that were kept secret. I saw how all of these themes echoed in my life and the lives of my family members. The entire ritual of honoring our ancestors surprisingly led to understanding myself on a deeper level and understanding that human suffering has one origin story that repeats itself in various permutations. These imprinted themes of abandonment, betrayal, rejection and fear in my life and my family's lives have had a long history of repeating themselves through different timelines and different incarnations. And the main lesson at the end of the day was to recognize the parallels of all these stories and what they mean in order to break free of these unconscious patterns.

Prior to my trip to China, my friend Fana, a shaman from a long line of African high priestesses, was guided to tell me to bring peace to the house of the dragon. This was before I knew my father's village in Yangjiang was called Long An Chun, which in Cantonese translates as "the village of dragon's peace." Somehow, Fana and I, though in different corners of the world, mirrored each other's experiences. She was simultaneously in Senegal clearing the distortions in her ancestral line under the banner of the phoenix.

She reminded me of the ancient love story between the dragon and the phoenix who were the perfect union of yin and yang. The yang dragon symbolizes chi and creative drive while the yin phoenix embodies wisdom. In the legends, the dragon would blow cosmic chi from his breath and was the expression of the divine forces of mother nature.

The interconnectedness of all the signs was remarkably synchronistic. December 2009, I encountered the International Council of Thirteen Indigenous Grandmothers at a healing ceremony in New York City, and through a divine game of roulette, we were randomly assigned the grandmother who we needed for our healing. Of the thirteen sacred women, I was paired with Grandmother Flordemayo, a Mayan medicine woman and sundancer from Central America. Each healer had their own unique way of balancing our energy fields. Flordemayo used the application of herbs and a gentle blowing of sacred breath onto my throat and heart chakras, which not only harmonized my field but also activated something within me.

After that experience, I naturally started using my breath to activate or release energetic patterns in my private clients in the way Flordemayo did for me. It was my own expression of using sacred breath for bodywork and energy work. Only years later during the ancestral rites in China did I realize the connection between that sacred Mayan breath activation and my connection to my ancestral dragon.

"If we think of the breath as a vehicle of communication that would center us, then we are not separate from the Great Mystery; we are in the motion of beauty," Flordemayo said. She very eloquently summarized how I feel my way through life and communicate with the unseen. And I truly believe that everyone can access this relationship with spirit through the breath to exist in an elevated way of being that is still very grounded in the here and now.

The beautiful thing about the ancestral ritual was that it wasn't done to satisfy our logical brain. It was done to heal our souls. Honoring our ancestors and paying respects to our loved ones, friends and teachers gives us the opportunity to nourish our souls. We express the inexpressible through the poetry of ritual, in the form of sacred offerings, sounds, and whatever else fills our hearts. As a teenager, when I saw my father pray over our family altar, the skeptical atheist in me demanded proof of what was happening. After a lot of fighting, I now have consciously decided that I don't need to make life so difficult by challenging the unknown. Instead, I can choose to live in awe of the mystery of the unknown. This was the gift that my ancestors gave me.

CHAPTER 15

THE PINK ELEPHANT
EXPLODES

"Awakening to your true nature is like a gentle hurricane. You have no idea where it started or how it found you. You just wake up one day in the burning heart of paradox, and realize that you are not a mere guardian or administrator of your life, but your own Co-Founder, CEO and Chief Executive Creator. Nobody, nothing owns you anymore."

ANDREA BALT

Traveling away and returning, traveling away and returning. It is as if every return to New York is a marker of how far I have come. In August 2018, a few months after the ancestral tomb-sweeping ritual with my family, I made my way back to America for the first time in two and half years. With all of my traveling, studying and facilitating retreats, time had flown by more swiftly than it seemed. The last time I had been on American soil was when Obama was president and gay marriage was not yet legalized. There was an anxious excitement about heading home again; I was excited to see my friends again and anxious about meeting my parents.

I became more and more restless as the fated day approached. Then it hit me. I would be bringing my partner, Andy, with me to

New York for the first time. He had never been, though I had been to Northern Ireland twice and had met his parents. Andy and I have had similar experiences with our parents not fully embracing our homosexuality. And though we share in this dilemma, the part of me that resists change felt my situation was a lot more challenging than his. "Well, his parents were not in the stage of denial that my parents are in. His parents are more even-tempered and civilized. His parents have had more time to deal with it." The list of doubts was exhausting.

I met Andy's parents on a trip we took to Kerry in the Republic of Ireland to our friends' wedding. We made a pit stop in his home in Belfast before driving down to Kerry. Thinking back on it, the whole situation was a comical experience.

It was May 2015 during the Irish referendum on whether or not gay marriage should be legalized. Andy had arrived a few days earlier. After a fourteen-hour flight, I showed up at his family's home and he told me very quickly before I walked through the front door, "By the way, I didn't tell Mum and Dad about us." I was not only delirious from the long and uncomfortable flight of shrieking babies, but now confused. *How do I behave now?* I thought. I didn't have much time to think about it as his mother greeted us at the door. We had an hour to shower, to repack my things and eat breakfast before our seven-hour road trip down south. His parents offered to drive, and so off we went.

To date, that was probably the most awkward road trip I have ever been on. Andy and his father took turns driving, and it took a while for me to acclimate to the politeness of car etiquette. I requested variety in radio stations, which was restricted to the classical music station because it seemed that all the other channels were talking about the Irish referendum. Though I didn't mind an enchanting Beethoven sonata, it was lulling our drivers to sleep. An hour into the drive, without many words, Andy's father decidedly switched the radio station off.

The Irish countryside was quaint and serene, so there was not much to distract from the glaringly obvious. Once we crossed the border between the north and the south, at every town limit there were hard-to-miss billboards with signs either supporting gay marriage or vehemently against it. It seemed like the perfect moment to drum up conversation. Instead, old-fashioned road maps were unfolded, and heads were buried in conversation about which route to take. Andy's parents were the complete opposite of my parents. There was no questions pertaining to my life or how we met. It seemed the unspoken rules for conversation were framed around the non-prying and impersonal stories of historical landmarks. I caught up on Irish history and learned how William of Orange won the Battle of the Boyne against the deposed King James VII who failed to regain the British crown.

The way Andy behaved with his parents could not even be compared to the way my parents and I spoke. I wasn't sure which one was more exhausting. For sure, Andy's family conversations were very diplomatic and refined. Rarely did I see heightened emotion. With my parents, every conversation is very emotional. Whether they can articulate it clearly or not in English, it is impossible for them to hide their feelings. Conversations in my house tend to get heated very quickly, and whatever emotions are boiling under the surface are always at risk of eruption. This was why when I was growing up, I seldom brought school friends home.

In any case, on a very spirited Monday morning, after a clear message from a dream the night before, without any hesitation, I picked up the phone and called my mother. I told her that I was coming home with Andy.

Our conversation in Cantonese roughly translated into English:

"Hi, Mom, I'll be coming home in a couple of weeks."

"Yes, when are you landing?"

"About that. I have something to tell you. Is it okay if I bring my boyfriend home?"

"Boy friend? You mean a friend who is a boy?"

"No, my boyfriend."

"You mean you're coming home with someone else's boyfriend."

"No, Mom, my boyfriend. Like as in the guy that I'm dating."

"Dating, as in you're going to marry him."

"I didn't say anything about marriage, Mom."

"Well, you said dating, so are you intending to marry him?"

I forgot for a brief moment that in Chinese the term *dating* is equated to courtship, like the mating dance between two animals— like when a peacock displays his bright blue-green plumage to attract a peahen before they decide they are going to tie the knot. At least, that's how my parents see it. They don't ever use the phrase dating, or boyfriend or girlfriend, unless it is going to lead to a potential status. To her, I was saying that I was bringing my fiancé home.

I could hear my mother carefully clarifying and defining every word I said to try and fit everything into her narrow worldview of right and wrong. Though I had come out years before, my parents reinforced their bubble of denial by holding onto the idea that I was a late bloomer and going through an experimental phase. It's why our phone conversations were every three weeks or so and very short, because it would always end with them lecturing me on the importance of family and children. One time, they even shifted tactics and argued, "If not for the sake of our ancestral lineage, then as an investment. Who will take care of you in your old age?" So, when I spoke the unspeakable, I could hear the carpet being pulled out from under her.

"So, that's it, you hate your mother and father so much that you're going to resign yourself to a life without children. You want to dig us an early grave?"

Her guilt trip express train was right on schedule. "Well, I don't know if I want children. If I wanted children, I could always adopt or apply for surrogacy."

A pregnant pause. I heard the wheels turning in her head. Nothing I said computed with her standard of normality. "Let's not talk about that right now. So where are you going to stay?"

"I was thinking of staying with Candy [my sister] and if you wanted to meet him, and do dinner, then we could do that," I replied. The irony was that my parents had already met Andy a few times over dinner with friends when they visited Singapore. They actually encouraged my sister to pursue him and felt that he was quite a catch. The irony is just too much sometimes.

In those earlier meetings, the part of me resistant to change kept everything under wraps for fear of how they would react. But it was different this time. The part of me that yearned to be free of the baggage of filial piety and cultural expectation won.

Suddenly, I heard my father's voice booming in the background. "If you bring this person with you, you will not step foot in my house. How dare you turn your back on your ancestors with this disrespect. You are committing crimes against the natural order of life. It's criminal! If you are going to continue down this cursed path, don't bother coming home at all." Apparently, I was on speakerphone.

The moment I had waited for my whole life finally came. I thought it would happen when I came out; instead, my parents devoted all their energy to trying to fix me in the most weirdly caring way possible. With the announcement of an actual boyfriend coming home, their illusion of me going through a confused phase of exploration was shattered completely.

I thought I would break to pieces or become overcome with sadness. After all, this was the thing I feared the most. It was my coming out, part two. The ironic thing about moving straight into the heart of my fear was that I felt extremely relieved. Even as my father shouted through the phone, I felt a deep sense of peace wash over me. It was a surprise and it was amazing.

My call ended shortly after his explosion. There was no sense in talking to him when he was so angry. I reflected on how light I felt instead of what I had imagined. This is what Patanjali means when he talks about freeing ourselves from the five *kleshas*, or "afflictions," of suffering. All the five afflictions of daily human suffering are tied to the fear of death, the unknown, or, we could say, clinging to life as we know it. Others might even call it the fear of change.

It was like all the times I had fallen from high places. I have an old issue with heights, which I hesitate to label as a fear because I don't want to give power to that story. The memories of the time I was pushed off a cliff into an underwater lagoon in Mexico, zip-lining without a safety off a fifty-foot drop in the Dominican Republic, and paragliding off a mountain in Nepal while facilitating a self-discovery retreat come to mind instantly. In all of these experiences, I was in a group setting that encouraged moving beyond my self-limiting roadblocks.

I had to work very hard to override that voice in me that was stopping me from falling. And in each of these experiences, I was exhilarated to arrive on the other side unscathed. As a result, I received a huge boost of energy. Physiologically, the body is under a state of acute stress. Adrenaline is released, which then increases our heart rate, expands our lungs, sends more blood to our muscles and dilates our pupils. After that, the pituitary gland releases the "happy hormones," endorphins, and cortisol to boost the metabolism for increased long-term energy. We essentially become high after moving into the heart of fear and receive a surplus of energy.

Then again, the yoga sutras also talk about addiction in the form of attachment, so becoming an adrenaline junkie, which is a very real addiction, is not the point. The point is that when we move beyond situations that are uncomfortable, whether they generate a little bit or a lot of fear, we can get two things: either an upgrade to a state where we are closer to our existential state of bliss, or, if we get caught up in a state of perpetual worry and stay in the fight-or-flight mode, our system becomes overstressed. Research has shown how excessive stress will lead to autonomic nervous system disorders like IBS, high blood pressure, headaches, and hormonal and immune system imbalances, which could potentially lead to autoimmune diseases.

My standing up for myself felt very similar to the times I had fallen from high places. Making it to the other side was a cathartic and beautiful experience. I would not say that I regret the months and years of waiting for this moment with my parents. I am a firm believer of conscious timing. For years, I knew that my coming out process was not complete, partly because my parents spent most of their energy in trying to forget I ever said anything. Secondly, even after coming out, I still felt as if I needed to tiptoe around certain topics with my parents.

In unabashedly standing my ground and accepting their nonacceptance rather than giving way to anxiety and fear, I came more into alignment with the core of myself. I didn't die. I didn't sink into a pit of unrelenting depression. As a son who wanted to be loved unconditionally, I was hurt for sure. On the level of spirit, I was unscathed. In the bigger scheme of things, I understood that this was the karma that me and my parents needed to overcome in this lifetime. It was a perfect match made between our souls across lifetimes of misery. Perhaps this would be the lifetime where this pattern of dominance and dogma would finally end.

We were home for my friend Zoey's wedding, and I didn't want to add gasoline into the fire. When Andy and I arrived, it was my conscious decision to keep my parents out of his inaugural visit to my hometown. I met with them after he had returned to Singapore.

Dinner with my parents was uneasy. My father usually scooped up a bowl of rice for me and pushed me to eat more. This time around, he stared down at the dinner table in a somber silence, as if someone had died. It was their idea of me that had died. Few words were exchanged all around. My brother was absent. If he were there, at least attention could have been directed to someone else other than me. My sister retreated into her phone to dodge the awkwardness of it all. And finally, when dinner was over, my father decided to address the pink elephant in the room before me and my sister retired to her new apartment.

Not wanting to start a heated argument, and knowing that I was not emotionally prepared for anything at this point in time, I offered to return for lunch. He agreed, and I returned two days later. Having not seen my parents since they visited me in Singapore the year prior, I needed some time to recalibrate. I forgot how much they triggered me to explode in unhelpful ways when I was around them. It was best to take a recess before things went down.

Lunch was held in a very similar manner. My parents are masters of structure and routine, down to the very placement of where I should sit at the dining table. I knew the pattern now. The stiff silences were moments where my father was in deep thought, carefully planning what he was going to say. My mother distracted herself with conversation with my sister.

The post-lunch continuation of matters at hand with my father started when he was ready. Just in time for his daily intake of the fruit he has after meals. He went on his usual rant about the law of nature, progeny, ancestral lineage, etc. It was like listening to an evangelical preacher on repeat. He even went so far as to say that I was a hypocrite for being a teacher of meditation and wellness when I myself was unwell. According to him, I had a disease. He backed it up with his interpretation of Buddhism and defended his worldviews tooth and nail.

Then, in the most diplomatic way, he suggested that if in my five-year plan I planned to take the appropriate steps to correct my ways, he would support me. He had helped me with a business loan, and I knew he would use it as a bargaining chip for my happiness. The relationships between parents and children in Chinese culture have been transactional for generations. I don't know if it was always like that, but this is something that I have witnessed across the board in the US and living in Asia. How is it that love is always measured by financial support?

This was a test of patience as I was getting riled up and having difficulty sifting through my strained database of Chinese vocabulary. I breathed. I listened. I waited. Then, I asked him, what was the purpose of chanting and praying two hours each morning to the goddess of compassion for me to be unhappy? I contested the purpose of prayer and suggested that the sign of a prayer working would be when one experiences peace versus outbursts of anger. He turned an intense red. Almost the red of the barbequed pigs they skewered during the tomb-sweeping ceremonies.

He came to the inevitable conclusion that I was not going to acquiesce with his ultimatum. That hurt him. He sat down in defeat, and then all he could do was yell and curse me into oblivion for being a wretched, disrespectful child. My sister withdrew into the background even more, while my mother tried her hand again at playing mediator. I sat in silence with the pain of unkind words and my old friend, Rejection. I went deeper into the sensation of pain, and I watched it. The logical thing to do was to leave. But I chose to sit for the next ten minutes on the couch observing how the pain of how my father's biting words affected my body.

I already had moved past my fear barrier by coming to my parents' house, so I had to remain steadfast in seeing it through. My sitting there in silence was not out of a need to show how unfazed I was by my father's words. In fact, I was very distressed and could not do anything but sit there and feel all that was happening to me. I imagined a life where my father and I never spoke again. I fast-forwarded to his funeral and pondered if I would or would not attend. I felt all the permutations of what the pain triggered within me. I acknowledged all the feelings of being misunderstood and rejected that it unearthed, and I embraced them.

In doing so, something surprising happened. I started to feel light again. I felt like a laser beam of light had zinged my physical heart, like the time I received a crystal healing over a decade ago with a healer from Australia. He held a crystal about three feet from my body and used the crystal to harness a narrow beam of energy into my heart. Both times, it was an uncomfortable experience, and for those moments in time, the lines of pain and pleasure were blurred, and I felt peace.

This was the biggest reaffirmation in conquering the story of fear for me. No matter the outcome, I trust in my resilience and innate capacity to move forward. Even after I left my parents' house, and my mother called begging me to come back to make amends with my father, I was still in my peace place. As much as my mother disagreed with my homosexuality, she disagreed more with my father's abrasive way with me and was afraid that she would never get to see me again. She told me that he had not eaten the entire day after that lunch, and that he was sick in bed with a fever. My father had self-induced himself into a textbook case of psychosomatic stress to the point that he made himself ill from holding onto his frustration and anger of things not going his way.

I turned my mother down and offered to come two days later for the Hungry Ghost Festival, which is a celebration that happens on the seventh lunar month of each year. During this period, it is said that spirits are able to transition between the worlds, so the Chinese honor and appease their dead ancestors with food and offerings. If anything can bring us back into balance, it is definitely a holiday. My mother lives for cooking large meals in preparation for these traditional gatherings.

It seemed that the two-day break between my father's explosion and the Hungry Ghost Festival meal was exactly what was needed. I don't know how everything shifted so quickly. But my father retracted everything. He didn't apologize; he simply said that as a father he is stuck with me and by default given the responsibility of supporting whatever it is I do, whether it's a criminal act or not. *Okay*, I thought, *this is definitely a surprising upgrade from where he was a couple of days earlier.*

In my father's eyes, I was still a criminal and unnatural, but I knew that for him this was a big step, even though he presented his support under the banner of being stuck to me. My mother added her two cents and counseled me against gay marriage for fear that my assets would get clumped into Andy's. "God forbid you die before he does. Everything you have will go to him." Practical advice from mommy dearest.

My visit home this time around lightened me in ways that I never expected. I felt unburdened and free from years of hiding in half-truths. I accepted the imperfectness of my parents even more than I had before and am content with the possibility that we will never see eye to eye. And I rest in the knowing that it is not my job to convert them, even if they continue spending all of their energy trying to convert me. My choice is to love them as they are, as theirs is to love or not love me as I am. If we spend the rest of our lifetimes together still disagreeing, at the very least we listened to each other, even if it meant accepting our non-acceptance of each other. The most important thing is that I expressed my truth, and I transmuted my pain story for the sake of my own happiness and the happiness of all those who might feel like me.

CHAPTER 16

Moving through Life by Shifting Awareness for Graceful Evolution (S.A.G.E)

"Your own self-realization is the greatest service you can render the world."

RAMANA MAHARISHI

In my past understanding of spirituality, I aimed to reach this seemingly far away concept of enlightenment. I focused on transforming negativity into positivity. It was about elevating lower states into higher states and correcting wrong to right. Currently, my understanding of spirituality is not about trying to be good or bad. I stopped putting gurus and spiritual teachers with followings up on pedestals and out of reach. Every day is a practice of letting go of expectations and listening to what is actually happening underneath the surface.

It has been engrained into our mental programming to find more of the good and ditch the bad. As an extremely moody person, I discovered that this does not work for me. We have been programmed to perpetually be on the go without taking equally important time to back down and rest. Our entire education system stresses the importance of grades married with this egocentric desire to outshine everyone else. Somehow, 100 percent was not enough; extra credit bonus questions were born for addicted overachievers. It's no wonder why anxiety, stress and depression are on the rise. About forty million people in the United States suffer from some kind of anxiety and 75 percent of them have an episode by twenty-two. (These statistics come from the Anxiety and Depression Association of America.)

The concept of the American dream has actually poisoned the well of our collective human experience. It is our birthright to live in peace, happiness and joy. With the advent of ultra-high-speed tech gadgets that disconnect us from emoting and feeling, coupled with the idea that we need to climb this illusory ladder to nowhere real, we are in fact destroying our chances at peace, happiness and joy. Now this is a global epidemic because the American dream has been transmitted overseas via global financial institutions and Hollywood, to promote a series of unrealistic and unattainable ideals.

America, the glorious land of the free in which my parents found refuge, places an absurd emphasis on ideals and individualism. I am all for having ideals and expressing our unique expressions of divine truth, but I am also a strong proponent of balance. It's like the proverb shared with us when we were kids: "Too much of anything is good for nothing." We know that eating McDonald's every day, drinking five cups of coffee or smoking a pack of cigarettes is overkill. Why can't we apply that to the way we strive for things in life?

I grew up hearing ancient proverbs from my parents. Since communism took away religion, my father was adamant in drilling Confucian principles as some semblance of morality into me and my siblings. Every Sunday morning, we sat for three hours in Chinese school on Mott Street in Chinatown learning how to read and write Chinese. And we did it through poetry and age-old proverbs.

My parents warped the wisdom of these ancient sayings as a way to control and manipulate.

"Respect for one's parents is the highest duty of civil life."
"Remember, honor your father as the sky, your mother as the earth."

I hated the concept of respect from a young age. Respect seemed
to be a privilege not earned but gained through the process of aging
into a bitter and over-controlling adult. From a shamanic point of
view, the sky and the earth have no expectations of me except to just
BE, while my parents wanted to be the personification of the cosmic
sky and earth and demanded we, the children, be their subjects. It
was all so ludicrous.

"A book holds a house of gold." "Do good, reap good. Do evil,
reap evil." Then came the parts about education and wealth. For my
parents, school gave us more knowledge so that we could be picked
up as desirable employees, make money, start a family, and support
them in old age. Anything outside of that vision was unacceptable.
We were expected to live in the confines of their agenda, and they
so desperately wanted a second chance to vicariously live their
projection of "success" through their children.

What about the proverbs that they left out? Like: "A diamond
with a flaw is worth more than a pebble without imperfections."
"Everything has its beauty, but not everyone sees it." "Choose a
job that you love, and you will never have to work a day in your
life." "Wheresoever you go, go with your heart." It was obvious that
my parents weren't interested in the whole of Confucian spiritual
teachings. They attached themselves to the limiting belief system of
what their life purpose was "supposed" to be. They were so skilled
at using only what fit their worldview, very similar to how religious
leaders splinter universal truths to fit their goals of power. But when
an undeniable experience completely shatters a belief system that
we are stubbornly holding onto, boy oh boy, will we be disappointed.

On my spiritual journey that is still continuing, I had to unlearn
years of history lessons in school. Years of information being shoved
down my throat and expected to be digested as truth. My fifth-grade
teacher, Mrs. Silverstein, taught us about the concept of Manifest
Destiny. America believed that it could massacre millions of
indigenous people in the name of freedom because God was on our
side. It seemed bizarre that we were supposed to believe in Manifest
Destiny when the next week we had a classmate's grandmother come
talk to us about the Holocaust. She was a Polish Jew who survived

the horrors of the concentration camps and shared her story via a translator.

America, to me, will always be a conundrum. I don't deny that it is a place of great freedom in comparison to the rest of the world. Yet, at the same time, this freedom was gained by throwing huge tantrums, in the form of rebellion, like a wounded child breaking free from his mother's kingdom. I always empathized with the relationship between the thirteen colonies and the Royal British Empire. However, I knew that if I were always in a state of revolution, I would alienate everyone and everything around me.

I see the collective story of a nation's past spilling into the daily lives of its people. It would be easier if I were blind to it, but I cannot un-see the detrimental effect of modern consumerism, the insatiable need for instant gratification, the mass depletion of natural resources with no regard, and the rise of mental health issues in America and around the modern world. As children, we adopt the societal imprint of "take, take, take," and are misled into believing we are entitled to be "the boss."

The truth about being the boss is that we can only be the boss of ourselves, and not over others. We need to embody the kind of boss that is aware, kind and forgiving. It is about being a boss who is not afraid of making mistakes, failing, falling flat on our faces, and picking ourselves up again. It is about being a boss who is open to the endless possibilities—the value of experience over belief and the unassailable beauty of genuine human connection.

Through all of my ups and downs, I know now on a visceral level, in my body, mind and soul, that I am extremely moody. If I had to compare my emotions to the waves of the ocean, my mood would be like the unpredictable swells of the tropics. I never know when a typhoon is coming, or when I will be riding the top of the wave or crashing into the break. All I really know is that I am riding the waves, and that my power lies in the choices I make—how I react to the waves.

Inevitably, salt will get in my eye as I fall off my metaphorical surfboard. I can either accept it or resist it; salt will get in one way or another, and I can only change my attitude around the acceptance of this inescapable fact.

During my twenties, I spent my university days studying human psychology through the lens of an actor. The words on the page became reflections of my own inner workings and a deeper understanding of who I am and how I should be—truthful, loving, and unconditional in every offering I make.

This voracious appetite to know who I was led me to the awakening of my senses with various spiritual teachers and disciplines. This newfound awareness to the metaphysical created a mania in me. Like a hungry piranha, I devoured every morsel of spiritual teaching that was presented to me. I paid close attention to yogic philosophy in classes and workshops and read voraciously. In my self-studying of spiritual texts like the *Bhagavad Gita*, the *Hatha Yoga Pradipika* and the Upanishads, I went through a period of entitled arrogance.

I spent too much time denying that my youthful years of ridiculous behavior were part of my spiritual progress. My old patterns of separation and seclusion were hard to break. I had so many questions and sought fiercely for answers. Over time, I grew to understand that these moments of unadulterated abandon taught me to stand my ground. They taught me to not give a damn about what others thought.

I learned where my edges were—important to know if I'm going to commit to living my life authentically. For me, knowing what's mapped and where the unknown begins, allows me to gracefully move into my discomfort. It is in the conscious choice of flirting with discomfort that I evolve as a *homo sapien* into what I aspire to be, a *sage sapien*.

I always disliked the term *homo sapien*. Though the root word of *homo* in Latin means "man" and *sapien* comes from *sapere*, meaning "to be wise," *homo* is also the root of the word *homogenous*. I am all for diversity in culture and experiences versus the monotony of sameness. So when I discovered that *sage* also comes from *sapere*, to evolve from homo sapiens to sage sapiens made more sense as the state toward which our collective society needs to move. My wish for our species is to witness the increase of wisdom arising from deep personal experiences that will then affect the transpersonal expansion of our collective consciousness.

Hundreds of years from now, I wonder what human beings will wonder about the humans who lived during this pivotal time in our history. Will they wonder about how we made our decisions? Our decisions to fight destructive wars that are, in essence, unprocessed stories amplified from our personal battlefields. In order for our species to survive, we need to shift into a new paradigm: a singular culture instead of segregated dysfunction.

My wish is that hundreds of years from now, human beings will reflect on how the reconnection to our bodies and hearts via inner wisdom saved us from ourselves. And that inner wisdom can only come from experiencing the truth of ourselves, which will usher forth a golden age more luminous than any we have seen before. An age where we each are empowered to consciously rewrite old belief systems passed down from generation to generation. An age where the only path toward salvation is to shed the obsolescence of the *homo sapien* for the radiance of the *sage sapien.*

Lightning Source UK Ltd.
Milton Keynes UK
UKHW041506160821
388947UK00003B/928